STOVOLD'S

MORNINGTON CRESCENT

ALMANAC 2002

ACKNOWLEDGEMENTS

The author of this Almanac would like to thank the following
Officers and Members of the Mornington Crescent Club for
the pleasure of their willing assistants:

Jon Naismith, Tim Brooke-Taylor, Barry Cryer,
Humphrey Lyttelton, Colin Sell, Iain Pattinson,
Neal Townsend, Ray Williams, John Garden,
Emma Darrell, Trevor Dolby

Special thanks to Miss Sigourney Boophus for the pictures of
her great-great-great-grandfather 'Little' Sid Boophus, the
Infant Juggler (above). National M.C. Champion 1860

STOVOLD'S

MORNINGTON CRESCENT

ALMANAC 2002

ORION

First published in 2001 by Orion

An imprint of Orion Books Ltd

Orion House, 5 Upper St Martin's Lane

London WC2H 9EA

A CIP catalogue record for this book is
available from the British Library.

ISBN 0-75284-729-5

Picture Credits

Aphrodite, the 'Venus de Milo', Greek, Hellenistic period, c.100 BC (marble) Louvre
Paris, France/Lauros-Giraudon/Bridgeman Art Library • *The Portrait of Giovanni (?)
Arnolfini and his Wife Giovanna Cenami (?) (The Arnolfini Marriage)* 1434 (oil on
panel) by Jan van Eyck (c.1390-1441) National Gallery, London, UK/Bridgeman Art
Library • *Judith and Holofernes* (panel) by Artemisia Gentileschi (1597-c.1651)
Museo e Gallerie Nazionali di Capodimonte, Naples, Italy/Bridgeman Art
Library • *Arcadian Shepherds* (oil on canvas) by Nicolas Poussin (1594-1665) Louvre,
Paris, France/Bridgeman Art Library • *The Nightwatch*, c.1642 (oil on canvas) by
Rembrandt Harmensz. van Rijn (1606-69) Rijksmuseum, Amsterdam,
Holland/Bridgeman Art Library • *Charles I (1600-49) and James, Duke of York
(1633-1701)*, c.1647 (oil on canvas) (see also 122474) by Sir Peter Lely (1618-80)
Syon House, Middlesex, UK/Bridgeman Art Library • *The Swing (Les Hazards
heureux de L'Escarpolette)*, 1767 (oil on canvas) by Jean-Honore Fragonard (1732-
1806) Wallace Collection, London, UK/Bridgeman Art Library • *The Gleaners*, 1857
(oil on canvas) by Jean Francois Millet (1814-75) Musee d'Orsay, Paris,
France/Bridgeman Art Library • *Dejeuner sur l'Herbe*, 1863 (oil on canvas) (see also
65761) by Edouard Manet(1832-83) Musée d'Orsay, Paris, France/Bridgeman Art
Library • *Arrangement in Grey and Black No.1, Portrait of the Artist's Mother*,
1871(oil on canvas) by James Abbott McNeill Whistler (1834-1903) Musee d'Orsay,
Paris, France/Bridgeman Art Library • *Composition in Red, Blue and Yellow* by Piet
Mondrian (1872-1944) Christie's Images, London, UK/Bridgeman Art Library

Design and layout by Neal Townsend for Essential Books
Printed and bound in Great Britain by Clays Ltd, St Ives Plc

LIST OF CONTENTS

To my esteemed and most worthy patronne
My Lady Charlotte de la Bagatelle
From her most humble and devoted servant
N. F. Stovold Esq.

    Upon receiving the intelligence that you have again grown weary of those poor pastimes indulged at court, and are taking no relish in Durts nor Ballyards, nor yet desiring to turn your dainty hand to Whisk, nor to abandon yourself to the pleasures of the Poker, nor neither the 'modern' sports of Monotony and Trivial Par-Suite, I was cast into a desperation of spirit I beseech you not to tax your noble brow by striving to imagine. As you will recall, this humble instrument has introduced you in the past to such passing joys as Up Jenkins and Down-ye-go, and it is with consequent pride that I believe that I can once again offer sport to give such vexatious frustrations the promise of mutual relief.

    There is a game called 'Mornington Crescent', which first I came upon within the pages of a low and vulgar Almanac of 1591 by one hiding behind the name 'Tobias Twonk'. The contents of this work are purest nonsense, but by diligence I was able to configure the lineaments of the game proper, and therefrom derive great satisfaction. I enclose my own copy of the Origin and Rules (17/6) and humbly request my Lady that I may dedicate this humble Almanac of mine own to your most gracious person.

    I think I'm free on Thursday. Are you on?

    N. F. S.

Introduction to the First Edition of the Mornington
Crescent Almanac, 1782

Romney House
Marsham Street
London SW1P 3PY

Hello.

It most probably won't surprise a lot of you to hear that we spend many hours playing the game of Mornington Crescent here in our committees and steering groups. But we don't just play it for fun. Not a bit of it. We use it as part of our decision making process, and many a crucial issue has been decided on the outcome of a game.

I remember once when an important vote hung in the balance. It was my turn, but Goldhawk Road had been played straight after Kentish Town, so nothing above the line was available for melding! I was stumped for a move, but then I heard the dear old bells of St Clements outside, and they actually seemed to be saying: "Turnham Green, Livingstone — Mayor of London." I turned with a smile to my faithful Puss, and said "Sorted!"

As it goes, we lost on that occasion, and the Islington Newt-Support Outreach Facility remains un-funded, but you get my point.

Devotees of the game will find this Almanac invaluable, while newcomers may find it valuable.

Cheerioh!

Ken Livingstone

PS Sorry it's a bit more than the four words you asked for. K

THE MORNINGTON CRESCENT CLUB
About the MCC

The Mornington Crescent Club was formed in 1780 as the brainchild of N.F. Stovold, National Champion 1760, and

The Old Pavilion at Lourdes

undisputed doyen of the Game. Its origins were humble – a group of like-minded pleasure-seekers seeking pleasure on the village green at Wimbledon – but it was not long before Stovold had set down the

definitive rules, and formed the Crescenteers into a Club. In 1782 he published the first Almanac, still affectionately known to this day as 'Willesden'. As leader of the MCC Stovold not only decided the rules, he also chose the colours for the members' blazers, tasselled hats, and socks, dictated the length of their hair, moustaches, teeth, etc., and selected their diet, religion, politics, and wives. To this day the MCC controls the game worldwide.

The Ashes
In 1882 the MCC engaged in a series of 'Test' matches against the Australian equivalent of the MCC (the AeotMCC). The contest took place 'down under' at Coober Pedy in a disused Opal Mine which had been specially converted into an Olympic-shaped Crescent. On that occasion, as on every occasion since, the Australians won. Sadly at the end of the 1997 series the trophy, a finely decorated Eucalyptus Stump, was stolen by the caterers, Derek and Fanny Ash. If anyone knows the whereabouts of the Ashes, or has any information which might lead to their apprehension, contact the MCC immediately. Thank you.

STOVOLD PICTURE GALLERY

The Focus Group of the Ways and Means Committee
pictured from left to right

Portrait of C.J. Homerton
Retiring Vice-president of the MCC
by M.S. Clipart (Special Commission)

A curiosity for the faithful
An astonishing image of Mother Anna of Widdicombe which
miraculously appeared in a Jammy Dodger biscuit, found at Bella's
Tea-Roome Tuckshoppe, Eastbourne, 1958

Boyle's Hydraulic Elephant
*On its way to being installed at the old 'Castle'
Underground station*

Etienne de Silhouette
1709–1767
*Believed to be the first black
Regional Champion (Home
Counties)*

N.F. Stovold's Original Cat Piano
*Preserved to this day in the Very Long Room.
(The cats are, of course, replaced as and when necessary!)*

MCC REVIEW OF THE YEAR
Compiled by Hadley Wood, Club Secretary

Well! What a year to (correctly!) kick off the new millennium! The 21st century was (correctly!) welcomed in on the stroke of midnight, December 31st 2000, and before we knew it, it was January the 3rd. We ticked off the days until the 17th, and then went on ticking them off until the end of the month. Imagine our surprise when February appeared out of nowhere! Like many sporting societies we spent February, and the time flew past in this neck of the woods at least! I have no doubt that, like us, most of you noticed the change when February turned into March – a month packed full of days from start to finish! As we expected, the next month to arrive was April, which promised to be a bit longer than February had been! However, May turned out to be a bit longer still, which should have come as no surprise, I guess!

Friends and relations no doubt all shared our experience on June the 1st when a brand new month began. Like all of you, we find it hard to describe our feelings on these occasions! June 7th dawned bright and early – a trend that was to continue for the rest of the month! We were ready and waiting for July when it put in its annual appearance, and we all thought it might as well be summer!

Well I see I'm running out of space, so there's only room to give a brief mention to August and September (more about them in the next edition – promise!), but towards the end of the year we spent time with October again – and not for the first time! Shortly before October 31st we were delighted to hear that November was on the way – it arrived safely! We rounded off the year nicely with a full, traditional, 31-day December! Who knows what next year will bring?!
H.W.

MCC STATISTICS

Player	Playing career	Games played
* Hodge the Plumber	426–442	5
* Brother Chalfont	556–71	1,743
Peg o'Balham	5/11/573	1
* Ethel/Bert the Undecided	676–98	22
Thrathulthrith the Throth	701–8	19
* The Beardie Venables	727–8	365
Thathelthulth Thrithelfilth	769–77	4
THE DARK AGES	–	–
Darren Longshanks	911–12	2
Antan Dec	913	813
Knut Tokswig	1016–35	34
* Geofric de Groynes	1067–76	174
* Brodric Crofferd	1153–67	476
Thomas A[lf] Becket	1162–79	352
Saladin	1190	1
* Sir Brandreth de Gyles	1224–38	3
Simon de Montfort	1245–59	2184
* Robert de Winchelsea	1290–?	?
* Piers Gaveston	1306–9	184
Edward II, King of England	1307–27	0
Wynton A'Dale	1330–59	987
Necrophiloctetes Apparatus	1379–98	♋
Bob the Lollard	1374–94	16

*MCC National Champion

MCC Statistics of Notable Players (Revised and Updated)

Won	Lost	Avg.	Comments
4	1	0.80	At that time only 3 moves were available.
1,741	2	0.03	Sponsored by *Nux Vomica*.
0	1	0.00	First recorded woman player. Burnt.
22	0	1	Mixed singles title-holder.
19	6	0.61	[NOT Thruthelthroth the Thrith.]
3	1	0.99	Allegations later dropped.
4	0	0.99	aka Thruthelthroth tha Thrith.
–	–	–	PLAY SUSPENDED [due to bad light]
0	2	–1	Champion by default.
813	0	1	Unbeatable, but irritating.
22	12	0.8	Barred from tournaments for laughing.
87	87	0.5	Retired [hernia].
406	8	0.19	Brought Law and Order to the long game.
213	6	0.34	Notable victim of Knight's Trap.
1	0	1	Defeated Richard Lionheart [away].
2	1	0.99	Owned Copyright until 1947.
2	2182	0.00	Lippy bastard.
?	?	?	Little is known about this player.
109	75	0.7	Often played for the other team.
1000	0	1000	By 'Divine Right of Kings'.
988	36	1.01	Played the 100 Years' Game. A recluse.
♎	♐	♑	Alchemist. Pioneered 'scientific' game.
15	1	0.97	Devised the game of 'Lob the Bollard'.

MCC STATISTICS

Player	Playing career	Games played	
* Snwpdorgg y Dorgg *[Welsh]*	1431–9	362	
The Earl Scort	1443–55	21	
* Perkin Warbeck	1478–99	73	
Werkin Porbeck	1478–99	73	
Warkin Wardrobe	1478–99	68	
Cardinal Wolsey	1515–29	1,473	
M.F.I. 'Kit' Marlowe	1571–92	193	
* Mother Anna of Widdicombe	1591–3	74	
* The Earl of Snaresbrook	1599	0	
* Hugo Mountjoy [Earl, OBE]	1600–1	166	
Sir Timothy Broke-Tailleur	1623–45	892	
Dennis Steme-Rowler	1646–65	302	
THE COMMONWEALTH	1649–60	–	
Nicholas Lymmpe	1650–6	0	
* Titus Oates	1676–8	3	
Porshan Beccx	1681–92	107	
* William of Satsuma	1689–94	2	
* Wee Airchie McSporran	1700–7	101	
Duke of Benson & Hedges	1708–10	49	
* Sir Edwin 'Southsea' Bubble	1711–39	674	
Lord 'Fips' Pipps-Poppinboy	1723–35	10	
* Jem Doenitz	1726–49	1	
Pitt the Other One	1753–76	133	
* N.F. Stovold [Founder of MCC]	1748–94	8,783	
Sir Nicholas Busby	1738–97	112	
Lord Knaresborough	1758–98	8,956	
* Lady Georgina Watts-Watt [First MCC National Champion]	1764–1808	269	

*MCC National Champion

MCC Statistics of Notable Players (Revised and Updated)

Won	Lost	Avg.	Comments
132	130	0.47	*'Crwssynt Morgantonio Llwciu'* var.
19	3	1.07	Fell at St Albans. Sued the Council.
68	5	0.99	Son of Gherkin and Jerkin Warbeck.
68	5	0.99	Man of mystery.
68	5	0.99	Son of Ikea, Queen of the Faeroes.
3,897	−539	99	Something big in gents' underwear.
931	319	1.93	Aka 'Tobias Twonk', almanacketeer.
74	0	1	Believed to have been stoned.
0	0	0	Bought the Championship Title.
143	n/a	0.79	Decorated for services to the Game.
891	17	0.79	Decorated for Christmas.
152	150	0.409	A Leveller.
–	–	–	**PLAY SUSPENDED BY CROMWELL**
0	0	0	The Infant Repository [perished in box].
3	0	1	Caught cheating and stripped of title.
1	106	0.0001	The Belgian Master [Bolton Grammar].
2	0	100	Cousin to the King: bribery scandal.
100	1	12.3	First Cornishman to win Master's Title.
3	1	0.25	Later the Duke of Marlborough [light].
374	300	0.47	Tended to burst under pressure.
5	5	0.5	The people's champion. Fop.
1	0	1	Shot himself. Sadly missed.
12	76	n/a	NB: <u>Not</u> Pitt the Elder or Younger.
38,789	0	1	Passed away during game [abandoned].
111	1	0.99	Court Player to King George III.
3	2	0.0001	Prone to lapses of concentration.
269	0	1	1st Ladies' Champion, captain of Hull City, and Pipe-smoker of the Year 1791.

Old Stovold's HOROSCOPE 2002

…What the future holds…By Gipsy Hill

♑ Capricorn
Dec 22–Jan 20

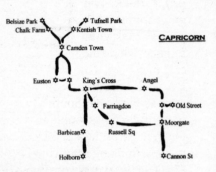

Beige is your colour. Your birthstone is Granite. Your lucky station is Kilburn. Wherever you go people will remark on your aura, but remember there are a number of effective products on the market nowadays. On Saturday June 25th you should order the *Poulet aux fines herbes*, but avoid the house wine. Romance is in the air, although the toilet accommodation on most commercial flights tends to be rather cramped.

♒ Aquarius
Jan 21–Feb 19

To Chinese astrologers this is the year of the Coypu, although to folk in your part of the world it is the year of the Wasp. A streak of extremely good luck runs from April right through to November, but it will not affect inadequate people such as yourself. Do something about your hair before it is too late, and take a long hard look at your taste in music. Attempting Venn's parallel out of Queensway will prove to be reckless and may cost you dear. Try to avoid Tuesdays. A Virgo will make a deep impression on you in October.

♓ Pisces
Feb 20–Mar 20

PISCES

Pisceans are not the cold fish many people think. You are a hot fish. Ask anyone. Ask your mother what she told me.

Riverside signs, such as Bank and South Quay, may appear tempting, but will lead to trouble if your approaches are open. Better to play safe, and stick to the Triangle. The cagoule you are thinking of buying in March will not suit you. Don't let this worry you: they don't suit anybody. While you're in March, why not visit the Cambridgeshire Nail Museum? It's well worth the visit, and you can purchase a wide range of clippings.

♈ Aries
Mar 21–Apr 20

Don't let people boss you around. That is an order. Aries is a warm water sign, which is reflected in your choice of beverages and hobbies. Financial matters will cause great concern for the foreseeable future and beyond, but just when you feel you are staring into a bottomless pit, you will find things start looking up. With the Moon entering the Circle Line, and Orion ruling the quadrant of Goldhawk Road, you must take care to avoid regressive Nip at all costs, unless the Tangents of the Seven Sisters are in your favour. Remember, Rams have horns, but you don't. If you are thinking of flying abroad this summer, avoid Capricorns.

Taurus
Apr 21–May 21

Your tendency to let your heart rule your head may cause you problems at work. You should also avoid letting your eyebrow rule your small intestine. This will cause you problems on public transport. Take care not to become too set in your ways; why not try the Pepperoni topping with extra anchovies for a change? After all, the wig fools nobody. Your lucky number has been changed.

II Gemini
May 22–Jun 21

Shame on the pair of you! Now is the time for making new friends, as making old friends has obviously not turned out well for you. Bad luck is heading your way, unless you make sure to order your copy of Old Stovold's Mornington Crescent Almanac 2003 in good time.

Cancer
Jun 22–July 23

People born under the Sign of the Crab may appear to be straightforward, but have a tendency to move suddenly sideways. Think very carefully before taking up that new job as a train driver. If disagreements with your partner should arise over sharing the housework, you will find yourself treading on eggshells. Be a sport and clear them up.

♌ Leo
July 24–Aug 23

Expect some sort of domestic upheaval between February 12th and 13th, when you will find the fire brigade are very friendly and sympathetic. You may experience some problems with a large company, possibly something to do with insurance. You'll find your finances will improve if you place a shrewd bet on the Boat Race. The winning team will be from a university town, and have an even number of oars. I see the colour blue.

♍ Virgo
Aug 24–Sept 23

During the summer expect to find yourself growing even fatter. Just remember the old saying 'Sticks and stones may break my bones', and avoid sticks and stones. As always, try not to wear tight-fitting socks at work. A long string of bad luck is coming to an end, to be followed by another. This will be a good year for you to bear in mind Farringdon and Latimer Road. They will not bring you good fortune in the Game, but if you contemplate their Western conjunctions regularly, you will find it soothing to the fevered brow.

♎ Libra
Sept 24–Oct 23

Resist your tendency to live in the past. Plan ahead, as far as this is possible. It may be worthwhile reminding your family that undertakers tend to get booked up later in the year, and early frosts can make the ground very hard to dig. Make the most of August.

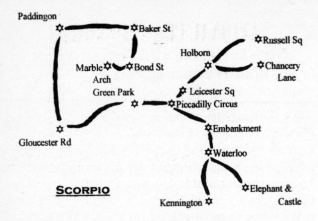

SCORPIO

♏ **Scorpio**
Oct 24–Nov 22

This is the year to grasp the nettle firmly with both hands. Stings, doesn't it? Now could be the time to invest in a pair of Stovold's Tuffguy Garden Mitts, available from most responsible outlets (£12 each or £23.99 for two). A difficult decision looms which will change your life completely, but you find yourself unable to make a choice between the two available options. The best date for making that crucial decision is either June 11th or July 2nd. You choose.

♐ **Sagittarius**
Nov 23–Dec 21

2002 will be a very good year for those working in newspapers and the media. They will discover your 'little secret', and live off it for months. This may be the year to take some time off from politics. Former friends will keep you in their sights. Your lucky airport is Gatwick. Your lucky fabric is Kevlar. On the bright side, before the end of the year you will receive a small inheritance from a Libran.

NATIONAL CHAMPIONSHIPS
Updated list of all winners of the Mornington Crescent National Champion Trophy Shield. AD 438–1301

AD 438 Hodge the Plumber
(First recorded MCC Champion)
A steady rather than an inspired player, best known for devising the Knightsbridge to Ongar opening, which remains popular to this day. Often cited as one of the Game's most convivial, natural and honest players, nevertheless a very private person.
Qualifying scores: 1–0, 1–0, 1–0, 1–0, 0–1, 0–1, 1–0, 1–0.

557 Brother Chalfont
An inspired rather than a steady player, he first came to the public's attention when he beat St Columba in a Pro/Monk tournament at The Belfry. He outwitted the Saint, who was 11–4 favourite, with a cunning Offside Trap, and impressed the judges with his gifts: a haunch of venison and a crate of mead apiece.
Qualifying scores: 1–0, 1–0, 1–0, 1–0, 0–1, 0–1, 1–0, 1–0.

5/11/573 (4.15–5.03 pm) Peg o'Balham
Peg began her all too short competitive career with Gloucestershire Colts, before graduating to the National Champions League, and playing against real people. At the time it was thought to bring bad luck if a woman took part in the Game, and so it proved for Peg o'Balham. Immediately after winning the title, she was burnt at the stake. Often cited as one of the Game's most congenial, plump and popular players, nevertheless a very private person.
Qualifying scores: 1–0, 1–0, 1–0, 1–0, 0–1, 0–1, 1–0, 1–0.

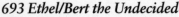

693 Ethel/Bert the Undecided

A steady rather than an inspired player, a popular champion, noted for a flamboyant style of make-up and choice of accessories. Often cited as one of the Game's most confused, androgynous and sociable players, nevertheless a very private person.

Qualifying scores: 1–0, 1–0, 1–0, 1–0, 0–1, 0–1, 1–0, 1–0.

728 The Beardie Venables

A steady rather than an inspired player. Often cited as a very private person. Also noted for having read the first novel written in English.

Qualifying scores: 1–0, 1–0, 1–0, 1–0, 0–1, 0–1, 1–0, 1–0.

THE DARK AGES

Play was suspended
(or if anyone *was* playing the game during this period, nobody saw them).

1067 Geofric de Groynes

A steady rather than an inspired player, and once the matter of his British citizenship had been sorted out, a popular champion and talented ventriloquist. His celebratory *gigot* 'Groynes's Clampe' is danced to this very day in Lowestoft. Often cited as one of the Game's most devious, unscrupulous and Norman players, nevertheless a very private person.

Qualifying scores: 1–0, 1–0, 1–0, 1–0, 0–1, 0–1, 1–0, 1–0.

1167 Brodric Crofferd

A steady rather than an inspired player, a popular champion, and a first class cudgel-man. First introduced to the game at school, then worked through the minor and county leagues before achieving international status. Often cited as one of the Game's most heavy-handed, confrontational, rude and yet popular players, nevertheless a very private person.

Qualifying scores: 1–0, 1–0, 1–0, 1–0, 0–1, 0–1, 1–0, 1–0

1238 Sir Brandreth de Gyles

A steady rather than an inspired player, a popular champion, sponsored by the Guild of Woollers, he dominated the Game for many weeks. Often cited as one of the Game's most bland, charming and inventive players, nevertheless a very private person.

Qualifying scores: 1–0, 1–0, 1–0, 1–0, 0–1, 0–1, 1–0, 1–0.

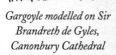

Gargoyle modelled on Sir Brandreth de Gyles, Canonbury Cathedral

1301 Robert de Winchelsea
(Archbishop of Canterbury)

A steady rather than an inspired player. Often cited as one of the Game's most controversial, sanctimonious, arrogant, intolerant, cruel, bloodthirsty, ruthless and yet popular players, nevertheless a very private person.

Qualifying scores: 1–0, 1–0, 1–0, 1–0, 0–1, 0–1, 1–0, 1–0.

DEATH ON THE LINE
An excerpt from the novel by Agatha Crescent (1938)

Chapter Thirteen

Percule Hainault twirled his moustache thoughtfully, then put it carefully away in its tortoiseshell case. He reflected on how the mood aboard the underground train had changed in the last few days. A pall of gloom and suspicion had descended over the passengers since the latest murder. How different they all seemed now in comparison to the merry chattering band of strangers who had joined the legendary Northern Line Express at the Edgware Underground Terminus, excited at the prospect of the days and nights that lay ahead as they crossed the whole of London – below the very Thames itself – to the heady and exotic sights and sounds and smells of Morden. How eagerly they had boarded the train, shown to their compartments by friendly attendants who took their orders for cocktails as the jolly troupe of porters loaded their suitcases, hat-boxes, steamer trunks, travelling bureaus and crates of ice into the luggage van. That evening, dinner in the Dining Car had been a convivial affair as the passengers got to know one another, and afterwards played games in the Saloon Carriage. As the train had passed slowly through Colindale, it was a cheerful company of travellers who retired to their berths for the night, tired but very happy.

Now, two days and fifteen murders later, Hainault sighed as he fastidiously massaged balm of Swarfega into his brow and cheeks, and powdered his teeth with Lily of the Valley talc. He slicked down his hair with a generous sprinkling of Pomade – an aerated apple drink which, despite the uncomfortable fizzing sensation it produced on the scalp, kept his hair immaculately in place – and then he brushed on a dab of mascara, the merest hint of blusher, and as a final touch, applied a drop of toilet water behind each ear before pulling the chain. Reattaching his moustache, he regarded the final effect in the full-length mirror on the door of the toilet cubicle. Neat and trim as a pin. Before rejoining his travelling companion Captain Harringay in their lounge compartment, he checked the crease in his handkerchief, ensured that exactly three quarters of an inch of immaculate white shirt cuff showed at the end of each trouser-leg, flicked an imaginary speck of dust from his lapel, and brushed a real speck of dust from his imaginary spats. He stepped out of the cubicle.

'Flies!' said Harringay as the great detective entered. Hainault hurriedly adjusted his dress, and sat down on a banquette. He leapt up at once.

''Arringay!' he expostulated. 'What an irresponsible place to leave your packed lunch.'

'I'm sorry. My mind's been preoccupied with all these murders.'

'Ah *oui*, my brave. I still feel we are no closer to a solution. But if you will follow me, per'aps we shall see what we shall see what we shall see.'

All was silent in the Library Carriage, as five worried faces regarded the diminutive detective who stood before them. Outside the window, Brent Cross station crept slowly past, unnoticed by the occupants of the deep leather chairs.

'I expect you are wondering why I 'ave asked you all to be 'ere.'

Five heads nodded in confusion.

'Let me explain. Tomorrow night in the Ballroom Carriage I am 'olding *une petite soirée,* and you are the only string quintet on board. Starting at eight thirty, two sets, M.U. rates – any good?'

'Fine by us, guv,' said 'Humph' Leytonstone, the leader, plucking a minor chord on his *trompettina*. The musicians filed out.

'Superb!' said Hainault, 'but first, my dear 'Arringay, you and I have a little matter to settle.'

'I can let you have it by Friday.'

'No no, you misappre'end. I refer to the so-called unsolved murders.'

'So-called? You mean you've solved them?'

'Per'aps. Per'aps not. Per'aps…per'aps.' The tiny but impeccably turned out foreign sleuth tapped the side of his nose with the end of his silver-topped Malacca cane, which made his eyes water.

There was little conversation around the dinner table that evening, the third night of what was proving to be an eventful trip. The passengers were waiting for the arrival of Tiger 'Sticky' Putney-Bridge before the meal could be served. At last he bounced in straight from the Tennis Compartment, in a good mood having beaten the resident pro in straight sets. She had put her defeat down to a particularly heavy schedule the previous night, but 'Sticky' felt his victory had been won fair and square. The trim waitresses bustled about serving the soup and hot rolls, and soon the party was tucking in with gusto, as the train bowled sedately through Belsize Park. It was not long before Lady Violet 'Gnasher' Ickenham began to unleash her customary stream of vitriol.

'Look at yourselves! What a miserable bunch of dross you all are. Here you all sit with a foreigner at the same table, and not one of you has the guts to protest. I suppose you think it's all right, do you, proper English people dining with a Belgian?'

Hainault bristled, then smoothed himself down and stood up.

'Your ladyship, I am not Belgian. I am Walloon!'

'And in what way is that better, little man?'

'Pah! Let me prove my point. Can any of you name one single Walloonian you 'ave never 'eard of?'

A satisfactory silence caused Hainault to smile and resume his seat.

'A cheap trick, Johnny Foreigner,' spat her Ladyship. 'And may I turn to your "companion", Captain Harringay? Exactly what is your relationship with this small perfumed Belgian?'

'Walloon!'

'I am his secretary.'

'Ha! Well we all know what men get up to with their secretaries. Up to the stocking-tops at the very least! And might I enquire of what precisely you are a "Captain"? The Wapping Ferry?'

'I am George Barbican Harringay, Captain in the Neasden and Kingsbury Light Foot.'

'Sure it wasn't the Light Fingers? I am still missing my mother-of-pearl hypodermic case.'

'I'm sure it will turn up,' faltered Miss Hangerlane, Lady Violet's companion and personal assistant.

'Shut your gob, Hangerlane!' screeched the aristocratic tyranness. 'You're no use to man nor beast, you bitter wizened dried-up sad pathetic miserable calculating vengeful twisted unstable shifty greedy conniving ugly hairy psychopathic ex-jailbird, in your lavender tweed two piece with artificial coral necklace, bakelite Victorian mourning brooch, hair in a tight bun, small round mean-spirited spectacles, beaky nose and sharp yellow teeth. And I don't care what I say to you, even though you do have the mind of a Borgia and the muscles of a gladiator. You don't frighten me, you repel me woman!'

Miss Hangerlane put her napkin over her head, and sat in silence, quivering.

'I say steady on!' exclaimed Tiger 'Sticky' Putney-Bridge gallantly.

'Ah, Mr Putney-Bridge. Always the gentleman. And yet, is it worthy of a gentleman to obtain his sole and not inconsiderable source of income by blackmailing his elder brother, "Pansy"? It was that unfortunate incident behind the Beer Tent at the Dar-es-Salaam Regatta which got him into trouble, was it not?'

'The poor chap was squiffy. He didn't know what he was doing. That was accepted at the trial.'

'Indeed it was, but I believe it was the fact that he knew *how* to do it that swayed the jury. He must be paying you most of his stipend to keep it out of the papers over here.'

Tiger 'Sticky' Putney-Bridge banged the table with his fist in anger.

'Now look here you wicked old…'

'Hush, "Sticky", you'll wake Mr Becontree,' cooed her Ladyship, teethed bared in a repulsive grin of mock reproof. 'Dear old Fred has been dozing again.' Fred Becontree, self-made millionaire, grunted and opened his eyes. 'Fred is very common and has no place here, but he is very rich, and therefore we are forced to put up with his company, however much we all hate what he stands for. The vile beast stinks of vulgarity.

Speaking of which, dear girl…' Here she turned her venomous gaze on little Midge 'Modge' McMonument, who sat silently trying to look pretty. 'Dear Midge. Still looking for a husband – anyone's will do. Always the life and soul of the party. I remember back in the Twenties you were a Slapper.'

'I was a Flapper,' pouted Midge.

'No dear, that was something else altogether. Monsieur Hainault, you may be wondering how I know so much about these creatures. I will tell you. Our paths have crossed before. They were all on a certain Charabanc excursion to Wolverhampton, on one of Becontree's Buses, with none other than Fred Becontree himself driving…or should I say dozing? He lost control of the vehicle as it passed my wayside menagerie at the bottom of the drive.' She paused to dab her eyes with a scrap of sandpaper before continuing: 'I loved that chimpanzee.'

'Frequently,' muttered Miss Hangerlane beneath her napkin.

'Since that dreadful "accident" I have done everything in my power to make their lives hell, but due to a typing error they are also all beneficiaries in my will – so you see they all have a motive for wishing me out of the way. But I am clever, and as soon as we finish dinner I shall sit down and strike them all out of my will! Every one of them!' She gave a hideous cackling laugh, and her head fell off into the soup. For a moment everyone stared in shocked silence. Then Hainault sprang from his chair.

'Fido!' exclaimed the sleuth.

'Beg pardon?'

'Name of a dog!' exclaimed the sleuth, clapping a brow to his hand. 'I see it all now! 'Arringay, arrange for everyone to meet me in the Pullman Conservatory Carriage tomorrow at…shall we say noon?'

'Noon,' they all said, dutifully.

'More soup?' enquired the waitress.

The hushed murmur of conversation ceased as Percule Hainault and Captain Harringay joined the assembly in the Conservatory on the stroke of twelve. With a flourish, Hainault removed a single rubber glove.

'So much for my chicken impression,' he announced, smoothing his hair. 'Now to business. I expect you are wondering why I 'ave asked you all to be 'ere. Oh, a thousand pardons! You five need not stay.' The 'Humph' Leytonstone String Quintet hurried out, much relieved.

'What we 'ave 'ere is a mystery, *mes amis*,' continued the perfectly groomed *oeuil privé*. 'It is mysterious, is it not, that the first fifteen victims were killed by a blow on the 'ead. A blow on the 'ead from an 'ammer, or an 'atchet, or a 'lunt instrument.'

'You can do 'b's,' prompted Harringay, gently.

'Or a *blunt* instrument,' the small detective corrected himself. ''Owever the demise of Lady Violet "Gnasher" Ickenham was a different kettle of boiling water. At first I suspected poison, but nobody 'eard the shot. Therefore, immediately after dinner I searched 'er Ladyship's apartment in carriage "–".'

'He said "carriage H",' explained Harringay.

'Indeed. And upstairs in the loft I discovered…this!' From his waistcoat pocket Hainault produced a thick polished chrome rod, about eighteen inches long, with a leather grip at one end, and clearly imprinted along the side were the words *Baltimore Blunt Instruments Inc.* 'As blunt an instrument as one could wish,' explained the short investigating agent, 'made all the 'eavier by the batteries contained within.' As he flourished the device his audience let out a gasp, and Miss Hangerlane licked her thin lips.

Hainault prowled across the thick Persian carpet from one end of the conservatory to the other. 'I think we may surmise that this is the murder weapon, and that the first fifteen murders were committed by none other than 'er Ladyship 'erself.'

'But why?' asked a puzzled Tiger 'Sticky' Putney-Bridge, looking puzzled.

'Because she was an 'orrible old 'ag, 'oo enjoyed inflicting pain and misery on others. And of course for the money: you will recall that all fifteen bodies 'ad been stripped of their wallets, purses, money-belts, and trouser-pockets.'

Fred Becontree awoke with a start.

'Money?' he grunted, before dozing off again.

Hainault thoughtfully tapped his teeth with a small silver tooth-hammer as he paced to and then fro. 'But we are left with the puzzle of 'oo killed Lady Violet, and 'ow.'

'Hang on,' said Tiger 'Sticky' Putney-Bridge, 'we all saw her killed at the dinner table.'

'Ah, but did we? We saw 'er 'ead fall into the soup, that is all. No, my friend, it is my belief that she was secretly killed before the meal, and the deed was done so cunningly that not even the victim suspected it 'ad been carried out. It was only the effort of uttering that 'ideous cackling laugh that dislodged 'er 'ead.'

'That's not possible,' cried Midge 'Modge' McMonument in disbelief.

'My dear young lady,' replied Hainault with a patronising smile, 'when one has eliminated the truth, whatever remains, 'owever improbable, is impossible.'

He bowed slightly to acknowledge the appreciative but slightly puzzled ripple of applause that greeted this *bon mot*.

'For this reason I say to myself – it is time for Percule Hainault to employ 'is little grey cells.'

'Who is little Grace Ells?' demanded Miss Hangerlane, eyes glinting like emeralds. It was Captain Harringay who responded.

'The "little grey cells" of which Monsieur Hainault speaks are neurones: dendritic cellular structures possessive of an axon or limb down which electrochemical neural messages travel throughout the complex reticular network that makes up the frontal cortex of the brain.'

'Pay no attention to 'Arringay,' said Hainault airily, ''e talks a lot of nonsense. In Walloonia, my dear, we 'ave a saying. So you see we are not ignorant savages. *Et voilà!* I set my little grey cells to work regarding the type of weapon that could 'ave been used to such effect. As we all know the sharpest blade in the world is the Gurkha military knife or *kukri*. *Eh bien,* this morning I left the train at Chalk Farm and paid a visit to Miss Margueritte Patten, this country's leading *kukri* expert. She assured me that no blade was sharp enough to sever the neck without the victim being aware of it, so I was left with that old favourite – piano wire.'

Hainault patted the sizeable piece of furniture against which he was now leaning. Those present exchanged nervous glances.

'Captain 'Arringay, kindly look in 'ere and tell me what you see,' said Percule Hainault, lifting the heavy wooden lid. 'It is a length of piano wire, is it not?'

'Well yes…but this *is* a piano,' said Harringay.

'What better 'iding place?' exclaimed the detective, slamming shut the lid. He examined his fob-watch.

'Excellent, we should be arriving at Mornington Crescent in three or five hours. I 'ave arranged for a policeman to await us there with a pair of truncheons and an 'andcuff to take the murderer in charge. That gives me plenty of time to solve the case.'

'Policeman?' said Fred Becontree, suddenly wide awake.

'Let us consider the evidence', said Hainault, settling into a cane and wicker easy-chair. 'An innocent piano wire concealed in an innocent piano. Not everything is as it seems. Nor is everyone 'oo or what 'e *or she* seems also…are they Miss Midge "Modge" McMonument?'

With a speed and agility remarkable in one so short stout and foreign, Hainault sprang forward and ripped off her false beard.

'How did you know I was wearing a false beard?' she cried, hurriedly re-buttoning her blouse. 'I was sure I had hidden it so well!'

'I think we've all had enough of this bally tosh,' interjected Tiger 'Sticky' Putney-Bridge. 'Surely you're not suggesting that Midge…' Hainault raised a hand to silence him: 'What I am suggesting, *mes amis,* is that one of you in this room is…the murderer!' On hearing those words, everyone jumped up and ran out of the conservatory.

'That's rather buggered up your denouement,' said Harringay.

The portly sleuth sank on to the chaise longue, deflating like a punctured Walloon. A slight movement caught his eye. His companion had produced from his pocket what appeared to be a matching pair of hand-tooled Purdey blunt instruments.

'What have you there?' gasped Hainault in dismay.

'It's personal,' said Harringay.

SENIOR MEMBERS

Trumpetmeister Humphrey Lyttelton recalls his first jam.

Students are the same the world over. That was certainly my impression during the year I spent as a lad on an Exchange Scholarship at the University of New Orleans. One of my first moves was to apply to join the University Mornington Crescent Team, known as the Basin Street Blues. What a crazy bunch we were! The team captain was Jelly Roll Morden, and he commanded a star line-up which included Billie Holloway, Count Bushey, Duke Ealingcommon, and Louis Amersham.

For a 'foreigner' like myself (my parents being Indonesian), it came as a bit of a shock to play the Louisiana version of Mornington Crescent – or 'Didn't he Ramble' as they call it there. One particular drawback was the limited number of moves available. There were in total three: Beale Street, South Rampart Street, and St James Infirmary. This precluded any kind of subtlety in the diagonals, and ground loops were inevitably met by a half-rolley and called 'out'. Nevertheless we struggled on and enjoyed ourselves as best we could, playing in smoky dives and hoodlums' speakeasies, as they were the only places at the time which served drunks.

It was in one of these low-life establishments that we first met up with another couple of reprobates who were hustling unwary punters into rolling high stakes on the turn of a pin. I never really understood what that meant, but they seemed to make a living at it. We would watch them fleecing the gullible from afar, until one night they introduced themselves as Django Ravenscourt-Park and Stepney Greenpelli. It turned out that Stepney was a fine fiddle player, though he had some trouble sticking to the tune, and Django worked wonders on the guitar, despite having lost three strings.

I suppose the big change came when another outsider like myself joined our little band of players. We first noticed him at one of our sessions, sitting in the shadows munching his habitual packet of Hob-nobs and tootling on his cornet, which was no mean achievement. It was none other than the Scottish genius 'Bix' Bide-a-wee. When we invited him to join the Game he declined, suggesting instead that we might like to join him in a musical diversion between rounds. This idea was greeted with enthusiasm by Duke, Count, and Jelly Roll, as all three played piano and had invested in an extra-large stool between them. Louis was a virtuoso on the satchel, and Billie Holloway revealed that he had a fine basso profundo, with legs to match. As for me, a wiz on the banjo, and thus relieved I was good and ready to play my trumpet.

It all seems so long ago and far off now, but that night jazz was born, and only two blocks away.

❖

STOVOLD'S LISTINGS A–B
Alphabetical listing of Tube Stations, showing number of times played as a move in Major League Fixtures.
* 2001 season *

A
Acton Central – *move played in 351 games*
Acton Main Line – 66
Acton Town – 1,943 (*a reliable blocker*)
Aldgate – 2 (*Cup-winner 1983*)
Aldgate East – 291 (*best avoided in Nip*)
Alexandra Palace – 17
All Saints – 12 (*9 consecutive weeks in the Charts*)
Alperton – 0
Amersham – 0
(*Attempted once at Blackburn Qualifyings, but revoked: n.p.R44*)

Angel

Angel – 544 (*Sunday League only*)
Archway – 543 (*still a misunderstood stretcher*)
Arnos Grove – 16,432 (*The classic Diagonal Opener*)
Arsenal – 1 (*Tuesday February 6th at Prestatyn Town Hall*)

B
Baker Street – 553 (*Irregular*)
Balham – 49 (*Disappointing year for Balhamites!*)
Bank – 150 o/d
Barbican – 1,999 (*see 1999 listings*)
Barking – 19,772 (*Popular favourite*)
Barkingside – 11 (*Unpopular favourite*)
Barons Court – 4 (*All played by TBT*)

Basildon – ? *(Awaiting recount)*
Bayswater – 862 *(Still only used in the Amateur Game)*
Beckton – 0
Beckton Park – 0 *(A regular move in the late 19th century, now out of fashion)*
Becontree – 13
Bedford – 97 *(Often confused with Rickmansworth)*
Belsize Park – 672 *(A crucial Bounding Gambit)*
Benfleet – 0
Bethnal Green – 15,674 *(Why?)*
Blackfriars – 44
Blackhorse Road – 783 *(<u>All</u> in October!)*
Blackwall – 1 *(An old faithful, seemingly on the way out)*
Bond Street – 1 *(Unfashionable nowadays)*
Borough – 51 *(Steady performer)*
Boston Manor – 0 *(Has not featured for the last 38 years)*
Bounds Green – 29 *(Of use only to the expert, hence the infrequent showing)*
Bow Church – 582
Bow Road – 582 *(The ever-consistent Bows)*
Bowes Park – 285
Brent Cross – 1,968 *(Shock of the season!)*
Brixton – 53 *(Local favourite)*
Bromley-by-Bow – 3 *(Often ignored, and rightly so)*
Brondesbury – 392 *(Not ignored often enough)*
Brondesbury Park – 12,837 *(The Bookies' darling)*
Buckhurst Hill – 1 *(A great improvement on last season)*
Burnt Oak – 22 *(No surprises)*
Bushey – 489 *(Frivolous appeal still apparent)*

Arnos Grove

THE ART OF MORNINGTON CRESCENT
The Game through the ages, captured by Great Artists

Mind the Doors!
(The Commuter of Milo)
Originally thought to be a product of the Greek school, c.100 BC, this sculpture was later found to be a clever 19th-century forgery. The shocked custodians of the Louvre in Paris were reassured by the Marquess of Turberry that it was 'no more than an armless prank'.

The Marriage of Arnosgrovi
Jan van Eyck, 1434
The excited newlyweds welcome guests to their 'themed' reception: yes, a stimulating game of Mornington Crescent is clearly in prospect!

Judith and Holofernes *Artemisia Gentileschi, c.1620*
In more rumbustious times, the Cheerleaders are seen here 'ragging' the loser after a Regional Final. All charges were later dropped.

Et in Acton Central Ego *Poussin, 1638*
Travelling Players try to resolve a dispute over Diagonals by consulting the Underground Map at the old open-air Chalk Farm Tube Station.

The Night Watch
Rembrandt, 1642
*The Tournament
Referee is called to the
court by the Umpire
after complaints of bad
light. (Play was
suspended, and an old
man led the crowd in a
sing-song.)*

Charles I with James Duke of York
Sir Peter Lely, 1647
*His Majesty and Yorkshireman James
Duke are depicted warming up before a
tournament with a quick game of Stone,
Scissors, Paper.*

The Swing Fragonard, 1732

Lady Eugenie Dalrymple is seen here distracting Lord 'Fips'
Pipps-Poppinboy during an al fresco session of MC in leafy
Kilburn Park. He was about to attempt the Cockfosters Tangent,
but lost his thread.

The Leaners *Millet, 1857*
Contestants in the North–East County League semi-finals enjoy a light–hearted stooping contest during the coffee break.

Déjeuner sur l'herbe (The lunchtime spliff) *Manet, 1863*
Drug-crazed workers from the Barkingside 'OK!' Bucket Factory indulge in an illicit game of Strip Mornington Crescent on Fairlop Golf Course during their lunch hour. (The men won, 1–0.)

Mum in a Sulk
J.A.M. Whistler,
1870
Whistler's famously
unflattering study of
his aged mother
portrays her in 'one
of her moods' after he
ruthlessly beat her
1–0, by using
Morton's Triplet
Ploy during the
Front Game. She
never played again.

Board *Piet Mondrianton, 1930*
A Dutch man's idea of what the playing surface should look like for
a proposed boxed board-game version of Mornington Crescent. Of
historical interest only, if that. (Mondrianton went on to achieve
greater success with his basketball courts.)

SCHOOLS RESULTS
2000–2001 Season

Accredited by the Oxford and Cambridge Management Board of Academic
Examination Scrutineers and Sports Invigilators. Sponsored by Olbas Oil.

Eton College – 1	0 – Harrow & Wealdstone
Dollis Hill Primary – 1	0 – Uppingham 1st XI
Baker Street Irregular School – 0	1 – Winchester '73
Finchley Central Colts – 0	1 – Charterhouse Wanderers
Totteridge & Whetstone – 0	1 – Marble Arch Approved
Chalk Farm Academicals – 0	1 – Stowe
Sloane Square Rangers XI – 1	0 – Aldwych VIth form college
The Angel Preparatory School – 0	1 – Turnham Green
Cockfosters – L	L – Shepherd's Bush *late kick off*
Fairlop School for Little Ladies – 0	1 – Barons Court Seminary
Sherborne – bye	Burnt Oak *closed for rebuilding*
Sir Arnos Grove's Academy 1	0 – King Edward School, Birmingham
Seven Sisters Convent School – 1	0 – Ampleforth
Foremarke Infants – 1	0 – Repton *own goal*
Arsenal – 0	1 – Barking Academy of
	Dramatic Art
Gordonstoun – 0	0 – West Ham
Swiss Cottage – 0	1 – Poplar Primary
Holland Park Comprehensive – 1	1 – Charing Cross Modern
Wapping Tech – 0	0 – Kilburn Incomprehensible
Timbertops Touring Team – 0	1 – Westminster
Morden Modern – 1	1 – Ongar Comprehensive

Mile End 'Nutters' – 1	0 – Rugby 2nd XIV
Tooting Bec – 1	0 – St John's Wood
Elephant & Castle – 1	0 – Fettes
Chigwell Special School – 1	0 – Oundle
Mornington Crescent Casuals -1	0 – Neasden
Mudchute – 1	0 – New Barnet Hairdressing Cllge
North Wembley – 0	1 – New Cross *after extra time*
North Woolwich – 0	1 – New Cross Gate
Kenton College	
for the Sons of Gentry – 0	1 – North Ealing Special Needs
Kew Gardens – F	F – Leigh-on-Sea *failed to turn up*
Northwick Park – 1	0 – Manchester Grammar
Kilburn Educational Facility – 0	1 – The Dragon School, Oxford
King's Cross Training Centre – 1	0 – Ladbroke Grove
King's Cross St Pancras – 0	1 – Laindon *stewards' enquiry*
King's X Thameslink College -1	0 – Northfields Preparatory
Latimer Road Secondary – 1	1 – Bash Street
Leicester Square – 0	1 – Lambeth North
Northolt – 0	1 – Kilburn Park *reversed on appeal*
Lancaster Gate – 1	0 – New Southgate *missed penalty*
Kingsbury High School – 0	1 – Benfleet Combined Infants**
Shrewsbury – 1	0 – Boston Manor

**The Stewards dismissed the claim that Siamese Twins had an advantage.*

SENIOR MEMBERS

Acclaimed Wit and Racketeur Barry Cryer remembers.

It was while I was appearing as Hermione Gingold in an all-male production of *Rosencrantz and Guildenstern are Deaf* at Radio City Music Hall in New York that I first came to visit the legendary Travelgonquin Motel. The old gang of wits were seated at the famous Round Table: the great Dorothy Parkroyal, S.J. Perivale, Robert Benfleet, Charlton Hendon (for some reason) and the Marx Brothers. Of course I had often rubbed shoulders with Groucho Marx before – we had both been masseurs at the Turkish Baths on 8th Avenue during a slack period in '38 – and it was a pleasure to see him again with his brothers Harpenden, Chigwell, Gummo, Zeppo, Boardo, Limo, Lido, Lipo, Brasso, and of course little Alan 'Titch' Marx. I immediately suggested a game of Mornington Crescent, and play was soon in full 'schlong'!

'Charing Cross' said George Orwell, in response to Churchill's 'Swiss Cottage'. His audacity startled some of the young 'uns present; Michael Jackson's face fell, but we all pulled together, and soon everything was more or less back in place.

'I'll be Beckton' growled Arnold Shoreditchegger while Albert Einstein took a pinch of snuff and jotted some calculations on a beer mat.

'Tee hee!' he cackled. 'According to my Gants Hill theory of Radlett-ivity, I go to Romford!'

Henry Wandsworth Longfellow looked up from the jar of pickled beetroot he was systematically wolfing, and waved his fork.

'Victoria' cried the poet, without missing a beet.

'What a bad move, you silly old man!' said James Thurber, as witty as ever.

At that point I got a call on my mobile phone, and as play continued I had a pleasant chat with Clement Attlee who'd called me to get a few one-liners for an after-dinner he was doing at the Ministry of Defence. In return he told me the one about the polar bear, and I in turn shared the one about the men in the pub, and instead of laughing he reminded me of the Repeal of the Corn Laws. During all this banter play had been going on, so I hung up and resumed the Game. I knew that my turn followed Woodford Allen, and after he came up with 'Archway' I took my cue.

'Rayner's Lane', I cried.

'Come off it Baz!' said Mussolini, with a wink at Jonathan Ross. 'Your outer parabolas are in touch, so you've got to chuck a Turberry, and well you know it!' Well that was the killer, we couldn't go on for laughing! What a night! I remember thinking, as I made my way back to Hatch End, 'Just wait till I tell the Pope!'

❖

NATIONAL CHAMPIONSHIPS
Updated list of all winners of the Mornington Crescent National Champion Trophy Shield. 1308–1700

1308 Piers Gaveston
A steady rather than an inspired player and controversial champion, he introduced the Game to the court of King Edward II and became a royal favourite. Often cited as one of the Game's most highly perfumed, unorthodox, flamboyant, graceful, flirtatious and popular players, nevertheless a very private person. Beheaded.
Qualifying scores: 1–0, 1–0, 1–0, 1–0, 0–1, 0–1, 1–0, 1–0.

1438 Snwpdorgg y Dorgg
(First, and last Welsh Title-holder. No other Welsh Player has carried off the title since Caradoc's ruling of 1447, limiting the use of sheep.)
A steady rather than an inspired player, a popular champion who worked his way up through the minor and county leagues before achieving international status. Translated Poggio's *Facetiae* into Low Welsh without success. Often cited as one of the Game's most misunderstood, incomprehensible, tuneful, wild and woolly players, nevertheless a very private person.
Qualifying scores: 1–0, 1–0, 1–0, 1–0, 0–1, 0–1, 1–0, 1–0.

1492 Perkin Warbeck
A steady rather than an inspired player, the self-proclaimed 'King of Mornington Crescent'. He later claimed to have been hanged. Often cited as one of the Game's most grumpy, argumentative, irritating yet popular players, nevertheless a very private person.

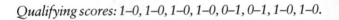
Qualifying scores: 1–0, 1–0, 1–0, 1–0, 0–1, 0–1, 1–0, 1–0.

1591–3 Mother Anna of Widdicombe
A steady rather than inspired player, Mother Anna flourished towards the latter part of the 16th century, and then became a nun. She joined the Blessed Order of the Mothers of Widdicombe. Unlike the Sisters of the Order of St Clare, who lived only on charity, and were known as 'the Poor Clares', Anna's Order refused to *give* to charity, and were known as 'the Mean Mothers'. Her game, mediocre at best, suddenly went into top gear after the incident of the turnip cart. She was MCC All England champion for 3 years running, a feat unequalled until the following season.
Qualifying scores:
1591 – 1–0, 1–0, 1–0, 1–0, 0–1, 0–1, 1–0, 1–0.
1592 – 1–0, 1–0, 1–0, 1–0, 0–1, 0–1, 1–0, 1–0.
1593 – 1–0, 1–0, 1–0, 1–0, 0–1, 0–1, 1–0, 1–0.

1599 The Earl of Snaresbrook
A steady rather than an inspired player, twice cited as one of the Game's most audacious, frequently arrested, and popular players, nevertheless a very private person.
Qualifying scores: 1–0, 1–0, 1–0, 1–0, 0–1, 0–1, 1–0, 1–0.

1600 Hugo Mountjoy (Earl, OBE)
A steady rather than an inspired player, he was awarded the Osterley Bronze Egg for discovering Hugo's Parabola, which had been devised earlier by Derek Hugo of Northolt. Often cited as one of the Game's most unpopular players, nevertheless a very private person.
Qualifying scores: 1–0, 1–0, 1–0, 1–0, 0–1, 0–1, 1–0, 1–0.

The Commonwealth Years
Play outlawed by Oliver Cromwell-Road and his
Purbiton Army

1677 Titus Oates
A steady rather than an inspired player, he overcame his
unpopularity as a traitor to the Crown by his mastery
of the Whitehall Straddling Vault, and his pleasing
baritone appearance. Often cited as a conspirator,
nevertheless a very private person.
Qualifying scores: 1-0, 1-0, 1-0, 1-0, 0-1, 0-1, 1-0, 1-0.

1690 William of Satsuma
A steady rather than an inspired player, this popular
champion was a minor historical figure before achieving
international status. He was connected to royalty on
more than one occasion. Often cited as one of the
Game's most peculiar, badly-dressed and Dutch players,
nevertheless a very private person.
Qualifying scores: 1–0, 1–0, 1–0, 1–0, 0–1, 0–1, 1–0, 1–0.

1700 Wee Airchie McSporran
A steady rather than an inspired player, Wee Airchie left
his Cornish roots at the age of three, and moved away
to the cottage next door. An unorthodox player,

he preferred to use a wooden spunt.
Often cited as one of the Game's
most aggravating, mean and popular
players, nevertheless a very private
person.
*Qualifying scores: 1–0, 1–0, 1–0, 1–0,
0–1, 0–1, 1–0, 1–0.*

'GAME'

A short story by W. Somerset Maughanington.

Strange things happen in the South China Sea. That was the headline on the front page of the *Straits Times* which the Reverend Ambrose Upminster was perusing over his breakfast, which he was taking on the deck as the galley had run out of plates. The Schooner *Goldhawk* cut through the blue water, under a blue sky, urged gently onward by a slight but completely colourless breeze. The Minister read on and, finishing the last morsel of toast, he took a generous nip from his hip flask. It was eight-year-old whisky, bought in Rangoon, and he grimaced as the liquor went down, wishing he had been able to find some grown-up whisky instead. To take away the taste, he took a swig of gin and tonic from his ankle flask. He would leave the rum daiquiri from his elbow flask for lunch.

The Preacher was tall, angular and austere, in a crumpled white linen two-piece suit and battered *chapeau de Paname*. He had been obliged to depart Kuala Lumpur in somewhat of a rush, leaving behind a number of unpaid bills and his collection of cigarette cards. The Reverend Upminster sighed, lit a cheroot, leaned back against a cat-harpin, and put his feet up on a stoker. His thoughts turned to Mi Lil Bro Dweh, the young girl who had been his body servant in K.L., and whom he had attempted to

convert. This tranquillity lasted but a moment. There was a commotion forrard, which he was trying to conceal as best he could, when suddenly the American captain of the schooner rushed across the deck, bawling. Drying his eyes the captain bellowed his orders:

'Batten urp the haitches!' he yelled, in his almost impenetrable yankee drawl. 'Batten 'em urp good and proper! Git ye battening! Squorl! Squorl!'

As all on board knew, the weather in the South China Sea could be notoriously fickle, treacherous, even cruelly thoughtless. Without warning, a sea as calm as a millstone could be unexpectedly hammered by a Typhoo or a Cycloon, the waters crashing about in forty-foot isobars, or lashed into a frenzy by a raging Doldrum.

'Squorl!' screamed the captain. The crew, lolling about the deck, sprang to their feet and then stood up.

'Whar be the squorl, cap'n?' enquired the Mate, above the din of deck quoits and parasols being stowed.

'Squorl behind the mere!' answered the captain, a piece of news which was met by gasps from the crew. 'Make for the nearest safe haven!'

The schooner *Goldhawk* slipped silently into harbour on the island of Dagnam, the closest shelter they could find, and before many moments had passed, the boat was securely nailed to the jetty, and the passengers stepped ashore. They would have to wait for who knew how long on the island, until the captain and crew had enticed the squirrel out from behind the mirror with nuts and pieces of electric cable insulation. How on earth it got there in the first place nobody knew, but as the captain explained: 'A squorl behind the mere do be powerful bad lurk.'

Apart from the Reverend Ambrose Upminster, there were two other passengers on the schooner's manifest. Mr and Mrs Ruislip were an upright, up-tight, and god-fearing couple of the Amish persuasion, en route to visit their son Toil-not-neither-do-they-spin Ruislip, who was a military man serving out East, based in Shanghai with the Midwestern Highland Non-Combatant Horse and Buggy Regiment. At first they had been perfectly civil to the man of the cloth, and at times seemed almost friendly in their quiet way. All that had changed since the morning when Upminster's shoulder-flask of Noilly Prat had accidentally tumbled into his porridge in front of them. Since then they would turn away at his approach, often sniffing audibly, or going 'Tut tut!' or muttering 'Bastard!'

Resting in the shade of a Pompelo tree, and sipping at a clam-shell brimming with iced toy-toy, Ambrose surveyed the situation. Here was virgin territory, and he felt his old cynicism slip away as he glimpsed an opportunity once more to do the Lord's work. He tasted the ripening fruits of missionary zeal, he smelled the imminence of redemption, he heard the jingle of the collection plate. What was more, the field was open, and it was all his. A thousand miles to the east lay the nearest of the Chalfont and Latimer Islands, a thousand miles to the south lay the tip of Luton-Luton, and about a hundred yards to the west lay the mouth of Hong Kong harbour. Dagnam was an island where the word of God had never set foot; the natives innocent of the Christian way, nature's children who had never seen a Bible raised in anger. He spat on his hands, and rose to begin his holy task: to introduce the Dagnamese to the teachings of the Almighty.

Leaving the bustle of Main Street, he wandered

through the relative peace of Other Street in search of lodgings. Within minutes he had found a room at the Hotel Habbakuk and his bags were on their way to his room in the hands of the smiling porters, Annas and Caiaphas, as he signed in at the desk with the help of the charmingly blushing receptionist, Revelations. That evening he dined in the hotel's Gethsemane Bar'n'Grill (last supper 9.30), and after a simple but filling meal of boiled meat, beans, and a mess of pottage, served by the waitresses Jezebel and Mary Magdalen, and washed down with a bottle of Naboth's *premier cru*, as recommended by the wine waiter Matthew Eight-Seventeen, he stepped out on to the veranda to consider where to begin his missionary task, and to enjoy a cheroot with Colonel Mudchute, the hotel's only other occupant.

Twilight in the tropics is over in a twinkling.

'What's that twinkling?' asked Ambrose.

'Twilight,' replied the Colonel. 'Don't worry, it's over now.'

The next hour or two were spent in companionable silence, save for the glugging of the brandy bottle, and the rustle of the brown paper bag as it was passed from hand to hand. At length the Colonel rose to make his way to his room. As he reached the door leading into the hotel he stopped, turned, and pointing a trembling finger at the Preacher, he whispered, 'Watch out for the woman.'

'What woman?' asked Ambrose, puzzled; 'surely not the chambermaid, little Deuteronomy?'

'No,' mumbled the Colonel, '*the* woman. Whatever you do, don't let her start!'

He was gone, in fact had been for some time, but Ambrose was given pause for thought. 'What woman could the Colonel mean? Don't let her start what?' he wondered as – the staircase being broken – he repaired to his room. He had left orders not to be disturbed. He had slept little aboard the schooner, due largely to Mr and Mrs Ruislip's nocturnal barn-raising activities. Nevertheless he slept but fitfully, and shortly after midnight he was awoken by a thunderous hammering at his door. He flung it wide to reveal the Night Porter, Corinthians, standing with a hammer in his hand.

'I just nailing up your "Do not disturb" sign Mr Holy Upminster,' he announced with a wide grin, revealing three rows of perfect teeth. The man of God sent the Night Porter on his way with a well-turned curse, then slumped back on to the sweaty divan and tried to find slumber. It was shortly after two that he heard a light tapping at his chamber door. Muttering imprecations he crossed to the door and once more flung it open, prepared to send Corinthians flying through the banisters with a well aimed prod. Standing in the doorway was a woman. Ambrose stared, quite rudely really.

She stood with one arm up along the side of the door-frame, the other hand on her hip. A black beret topped her cascade of bottle-blonde locks, her eye make-up dark but intriguingly garish. A lighted cheroot hung from her scarlet lips, her green and black striped jumper looked set to pop, cinched in at the waist by a broad black silver-buckled belt above a short skirt which finished a good inch above her hips, revealing black fishnet stockings clearly suspended by black suspenders, her long legs ending in a pair of shiny pillar-box red patent leather shoes with six-inch heels. Admiring her gold-coloured ankle bracelet, Ambrose looked her up and down. A Sister from one of the more relaxed Orders, he surmised.

'And who might you be?' he enquired.

'Ain't you heard of me, ducky?' she murmured huskily. 'I'm a game girl I am!'

Ambrose saw at once the kind of woman she was, and slammed the door shut, after waiting politely until she had come into his room.

Dawn in the tropics comes up like thunder. To this day, no one has worked out quite why a sunrise should be so noisy, but there it is. Ambrose came down for breakfast looking haggard and with dark rings under his ears. He joined the Colonel at the table farthest from the window, and ravenously polished off a plate of Grape Nuts. Colonel Mudchute eyed him closely.

'You've met her then,' he said, 'the woman?'

'I suppose I did, yes,' replied Ambrose vaguely, addressing the fry-up laid before him. 'I'm not sure I caught her name.'

'Miss Sadie Tottenham!' hissed the Colonel, 'and I can see she's got her claws into you now.'

Ambrose chose not to reply, instead pushing what he took to be a mushroom to the side of his plate, whence it scurried back and hid under the fried bread.

'Take it from me,' confided the Colonel, ordering another pot of Cinzano, 'she's trouble. Last fella she hooked lost his mind. Went native. Yes, terrible business, that. Going native.' The Colonel shook his head sadly as he parted his sarong to adjust his penis-gourd. Mr and Mrs Ruislip, the Amish couple at the next table, averted their eyes and started singing hymns and making furniture.

'I suppose she's still on the game?' supposed the old military man. Ambrose nodded. 'Thought so. How far did you get?'

Ambrose clasped his hands as if in prayer, screwed

shut his eyes, and in a tortured, strangulated half whisper he confessed: 'Liverpool Street.'

'Dear God, man! On a first date?'

'I am but a weak vessel!' sobbed the Minister, pushing aside his untasted breakfast, largely because the egg had winked at him again, and was now nibbling at the bacon. The room had grown suddenly silent. Looking up, Ambrose saw her at the top of the stairs. Miss Sadie Tottenham. With a sardonic smile, and a toss of her curls, she slid down the banisters, and swept across the dining room. She had chosen to use a small besom made of palm fronds. As she passed his table, she whispered to Ambrose: 'Baron's Court,' and then she was gone.

'Did she say "Baron's Court"?' said Jezebel, balancing a tray of pang-pangs *en croute*. 'In that case, Finchley Central!' and she let out a tinkling laugh, due to an unfortunate weakness of the pelvic floor. Murmurs spread around the room and nodding heads filled the air. The Colonel turned to the window and grimly scanned the darkening clouds. 'I was afraid of this,' he muttered. 'It's beginning…' 'What is?' asked Ambrose. 'The Gamey Season. Once that starts you'll be stuck on this island for weeks. With…her.'

Ambrose gulped.

Lightning flickered on the horizon and thunder growled somewhere far off, but not far enough. The schooner *Goldhawk* bobbed about in the little harbour like a cork in a little harbour. The crew were busily tying everything they could to the deck, including their feet. 'When the weather breaks, that's when it starts. They all stay indoors and…play.'

'Play what?' asked Ambrose, already knowing the answer he dreaded to hear.

'The Game! The damned Game you just started with

that woman!' snapped the Colonel.

'Dear Heaven!' cried Ambrose. 'What have I done?'

The Games were relentless. They went on unceasingly day and night for day after day and night after night, which is an unusual sequence, even in the South China Sea. The corrugated iron roofs rattled with cries of 'Leicester Square', 'Mordern', 'That's a diagonal!', 'Beckton Park' and 'Ongar!' It was merciless, and again and again the Reverend Ambrose Upminster and Miss Sadie Tottenham found themselves thrown together, usually by the Colonel and the Ruislips, often helped by Corinthians. Whenever the couple tore themselves apart, the others would throw them together again. They were dreadfully bruised. On and on went the Games, all over the island; the whole population suffered, and there was no escape. No escape, that is, until one morning when Ambrose stood desolate on the harbour wall, watching the schooner *Goldhawk* disappear over the horizon, having slipped away during a brief lull between 'Oxford Circus' and 'Dollis Hill!'.

In time the Gamey Season passed as it always did, but Ambrose went on preaching, preaching as he had never preached before. The Reverend Ambrose Upminster never left the island of Dagnam. Mind you, everybody else did.

WHAT THEY PLAY FOR
Some of the Major Trophies awarded at County Level

A miniature replica of the Vimto Lancashire All-Comers' Trophy, designed by R. Williams, Plumber's Merchants (Bath). Here it is seen proudly displayed by H.G. Crewe, winner 1959. The Trophy itself is on permanent show at 'World of Non-Ferrous Metal' in Southport. View by appointment only.

Amateur champion Ted Dunt admires the East Anglia Regional Winner's Stick. Ted was placed a creditable 73rd, narrowly pipped by his cousins.

A touch of Glamour! The Hon. Mrs Sylvia Wyndham-Coutts prepares to present the Horniman's Gold Cup, Silver Teapot, and Bronze Pail at the Hackney Regatta. Incidentally, her son Piers carried off the Gold trophy for the second year running, but he was apprehended outside the Cocktail Tent.

MCC STATISTICS

Player	Playing career	Games played
*Sir Evelyn Watts-Watt	1800–01	31
Admiral Lord Nelson	1800–05	111
Jack Camden	1803–18	276
Beau Wyndeau	1806–28	982
Asmodeus Morton	1806–31	5,923
*Adam Trouble Adams	1807–32	48
Nicholas Parsons	1809–41	0
Hugh 'Irish' Grue	1806–39	1
Captain James O'Sheaugh	1809–12	782
Colonel Thomas Crapper	1810–18	16
*Sir Eric Threepin-Plugg	1829–57	100
Charles Dickens	1836–63	1,201
Roofless Ned	fl 1848	n/a
Ethan Janks	1854–67	11,893
V.P. Cholmondley-Bolmondley	1855–56	1
Lewis Carroll	1854–82	threnteen
Damien Hobb	1859–88	666
*'Little' Sid Boophus	1845–97	0.08
Bridget the Tweeny	1861	2
Karl Benz/Gottlieb Daimler	1865–74	365
Marquess of Turberry	1873–87	912
*Dr W.G. Grace	1876–98	1
Barry Cryer	1894–	54,928
Lord Alfred Douglas	1895–99	6

*MCC National Champion

MCC Statistics of Notable Players (Revised and Updated)

Won	Lost	Avg.	Comments
0	31	–0.0	Inherited title from his father, Georgina.
111	0	111	Badly hurt attempting Pye's tack.
271	5	0.888	'Mad, bad, and dangerous to kick'
423	2	13	Fop.
5,924	5,925	5,926	Devised Hopkin's constriction.
73	0	1.87	'Trouble' was his middle name.
0	0	0	Not 'Nicholas Parsons', comedy legend.
342	6	y	Introduced Probation to the game. (Wig).
1	781	0.00	Fought at Waterloo. Arrested.
16	2	9	Inventor of the Waterloo Bend
90	10	0.9	Pioneered Gas Lighting.
1,200	1[to LC]	0.99998	Appeared as 'The Portsea Pug'.
n/a	n/a	n/a	A poor vagrant, and a worse player.
1,892	0.75	1+	Idiot. Went to Australia.
1	0	0	Fine player, unpleasant man.
poot	blang	π	The snurksome Bleeg of Glatter-throom.
660	6	0.666	'The Dagenham Demon'.
6.06	0.02	0.07	A mere 4ft tall when sober.
1	1	0.5	The toast of the Servants' Hall.
365	0	1	International doubles semi-finalists.
903	1	0.9799	Formulated 'Turberry Rules'.
			Fled to Tangiers.
draw	–	0	Man of the match. (see footnote)
12	54,916	0	Took up the game late in life.
5	1	x	The 'Bad Lad of Reading Gaol'

Footnote

*Not to be confused with Florence Darling, the Swedish Nightingale,
one-time mistress of Edward VIII (also not to be confused with
Grace Nightingale, 'The Lady with the Lighthouse').*

MCC STATISTICS

Player	Playing career	Games played
⁺ Humphrey 'Humph' Lyttelton	1893–	68,934
⁺ Ernie Oldiron	1900–07	talk
Mr 'Blister' Lister	1902–16	6
Mr 'Blister' Lister's Sister	1909–17	6
Dennis Howitzer	1914–18	6–4
Martha Farquhar	1903–18	191
* Arthur 'Boy' Allbright	1912–29	87
Wallis Simpson	1928–36	5
⁺ 'Tinker' Beaumont VC	1923–49	1984
Max Miller	1942–51	86
Max Miller junior	1952–61	86
Douglas 'Dumper' Wallace	1931–62	574
W. Rushton	1949–96	48,228
E. Aaron Presley	1972–	21
Dr Victor Birkenhayre	19??–??	7
Brooke-Taylor, T.	1948–	37,926
Gustav Penegar	1958–75	2
⁺ Zappa 'Moon-Petal' Tripp	1957–	1 million
Graham Garden	1959–	29,487
⁺ L/Cpl Tommy 'Goose' Green	1978–89	1
Annabel Lecter	1981–	8
Piers Tazza-Pharte	1980–	13
The Duchess of Chorleywood	1987–	240
⁺ Gryigoryi Efyimovyich Ryudetskyi	2000–	8

*MCC National Champion

MCC Statistics of Notable Players (Revised and Updated)

Won	Lost	Avg.	Comments
68,933	1	0.99999	Trumpet player with Radiohead
horn	big	Lauren	The Cockney Scamp. [see footnote]
5	1	0.83	Amateur.
0	6	–0	Very amateur
6–2	7–5	deuce	Inventor of the bayonet.
101	90	0.501	Singer, notorious for her colourful Wraps
63	21	0.249	Famed for his Opening
3	2	0.4	Willowy American chap. Went abroad
1939	45	0.923	War hero and itinerant pot-mender.
75	11	0.126	'There'll never be another!'
75	11	0.126	[See above.]
287	287	very	Air Vice-Marshall and bon-viveur
48,203	n/a	0.97998	Never took the game seriously enough
0	21	0	Tesco shelf-stacker [Chelmsford]
7	0	1	Socialite and bon-vivisecteur
3	secret	?	Facing relegation again
1	1	0.5	Lazy git
1 billion	1 zillion	1 squillion	Flippant hippy-type. Ghastly.
1,111	28,376	0.0334	[Spelt 'Graeme'.] Excellent loser.
1	0	1	A very physical player
8	0	8	A bit of a man-eater
0	13	0	A talented but unlucky player.
24	216	10‰	The Queen of Herts [and parts of Beds]
2	6	025	All England Champion [runner-up]

Footnote:

Cockney Rhyming Lemon (lemon = lemon meringue = slang) talk = talk dirty = 30, horn = horn of plenty = 20, big = Big Ben = 10, Lauren = Lauren Bacall = 0

MORN-ING-TON CRES-CENT
READ-ING SO-CI-E-TY
BOOK REVIEWS

Some recent publications that may be of particular interest to enthusiasts of the Game who are looking for a pleasant way to while away the time between moves.

The Little Book of Clapham
by Brent Cross
The definitive guide to discovering tranquillity below the line. The ideal gift for the man who hasn't got it.
'I could not wait to put it down.' Nick Hornsey.
Pingu Books

F*ing Shui for Commuters
by Lawrence Sewellyn-Ewing
The Master explains the mystical Eastern Art of enhancing the Positive Energy and Good Luck in your personal space as you travel about on Public Transport. When journeying on the Underground, it is a good idea to collect the strap-hangers' handles and display them in clusters by a north-facing window; place a trough of water across each doorway; unscrew the seating, paint it green, and rearrange it to face Finsbury Park, then sweeten the air by smoking a pipe of patchouli shag. Buses should always face south, and of course you must brick up all their east-facing doors to keep out the Bad-Luck Dragons! Follow these and many other tips and you will reach your destination refreshed, and having cleansed your inner *'pu'*.
Doubledutch Books

Skidmarks of the Gods
by Herbert van Luniken

In this, the long-awaited sequel to his best-selling *Mornington Crescent of the Gods*, van Luniken finds yet more traces of an alien civilisation that once visited our planet. He chillingly reveals that weird and threatening alien beings still lurk among us, and take special pleasure in sitting next to us on the Tube.

Little Brown (Jugs of Distinction)

"What a curious ending this Roman Centralion displays on the top tip of his Staff! Is it not a reminder of the strange cymbal seen outside every Underground Station in the ground? Yes it is! I call it eary! The Staff was used in ceremonies no doubt, but there is evidence it was also used in ritual forms of warfare, known as Staff Disputes. Uncanny!"

Herbert van Luniken

Notes from a Short Platform
by Bill Bryxton

Invertebrate traveller Bill Bryxton takes a cock-eyed look down the up escalator at the Metropolitan Underworld we all take for granted below our feet. Lovers of a good laugh will keep turning the pages. His tales of crowded, unpunctual, uncomfortable and unclean trips on the Tube spring fresh-minted from the page, although his attitude may be a little too American for some tastes. Anyone who was wondering if this author was running out of ideas will find their answer here.

Hodder or Stoughton

Bitch Volleyball
by Jilly Hooter
Once again Jilly applies her cutting wit, sardonic eye, and familiar cast of characters and plotlines to the latest sporting sensation. A trip on the Bikini Line will never be the same again.
'*I laughed so much, I fell off my chair!*' Jilly Hooter.
Chalfont & Latimer

The St Legume Handicap
by John McRidiclus
The true history of the legendary classic event for three-year-old Peas, Beans, and Lentils. One to set the pulses racing.
Sporting Loaf Books

Underground Gardening
by Alan Titsman and Charley Divot
This is horticulture from the bottom up! Join that popular pair Charley as Alan takes her below the sod to poke their bulbs and seeds up into the roof, and later on pluck the dangling potatoes, eye-watering onions, and groaning turnips that festoon the vaults of their subterranean grotto. Illustrated with two colour photos.
O'Rion Books, Tralee

Charley prepares to tackle a dangling pair of veg.

Harry Poplar and the Crescent of Mornington
by J.K. Rollingstock

Poor old Harry's in trouble again! The evil Vordermant has kidnapped Boxing Day, and it's up to Harry and his chums to get it back and return it to the BBC. All the Hogwash favourites are here: Headmaster Dimblebumbee (with the scar above his left knee which is a perfect map of the London Underground), Professor MacGonadall, Ainsley Hagriot, Snat, Pilch, Step-Henfry, Ophelia Dickson-Wright and Kirsty Wark. The Panoramal action builds to a terrific climax during an exciting Shoreditch contest. Without doubt this is a book that will be enjoyed by all children from 7 to five past.

Harry test-drives the Nimvax 300

True NecRomance

Carol Vorderman's Book of Numbers

Continuing the series that began with *Carol Vorderman's Book of Genesis*, this is a worthy follow-up to her Leviticus. One can only marvel at the depth of her scholarship, and wonder where on earth she gets her ideas from. A deeply enriching book for its author.

Octopus Press free with every copy purchased

SENIOR MEMBERS

The MCC's residual medico, Dr Graeme Garden, shares a few light-hearted thoughts on the life-threatening nature of the Game.

Many people who are unfamiliar with the Game think of it as no more than a gentle and harmless pastime. How wrong they are! Mornington Crescent is right up there at the top of the Dangerous Sports League, along with Deep-Sea Driving, Budgie Jumping and Free-fall Parakeeting. Number One for fatalities during play is still Crown Green Bowling of course, but this is statistically due to the elderly nature of the players, and the fact that they are at that stage of life when tempers are short, and there is a tendency to lash out. They also have a ready supply of 1.5 kg wooden bowls at hand.

Nevertheless, Mornington Crescent is not without its hazards. Many is the time I have been called to the touchline after a player has plunged into a vigorous game too soon after a heavy meal. In addition to the obvious risks of over-exertion and the trauma inherent in all contact sports, there are other less obvious dangers that should always be borne in mind:

Stanmore has sharp edges which can inflict serious injury if handled carelessly.

Plaistow is dangerous if swallowed by small children. Always check the insulation before approaching *Limehouse*, and be sure to wear rubber-soled socks.

Be sensible and use a stepladder; never stand on an unsupported *Hyde Park Corner* to reach *Ickenham*.

The *Claphams, North & South*, are the only pair breeding in captivity, and can become extremely aggressive if approached when guarding their young.

Hackney Wick has small parts which should not be put in the mouth.

Parson's Green is toxic.

Gospel Oak can cause an irritating skin rash.

Never turn your back on *Hadley Wood*. It also makes sense to have a First Aid kit close to the playing area, and this should contain bandages, plasters, lint, a proprietary bas-relief cream, antiseptic, tranquilliser darts, morphine, splints, paracetamol, and an ambulance. These simple precautions should ensure the safety of the players, and enjoyment for all.

In conclusion then, if there is one cardinal rule in preparing adequately for a safe session of Mornington Crescent it is, quite simply, to ensure that you always…(couldn't make out the Doc's handwriting here, Ed. Typical, eh? Can you check it out before we go to press? Ta! Yrs Jim the Typesetter.)…not forgetting the hat.

If nothing else, bear in mind the legend emblazoned above the entrance to the MCC Branch Headquarters at Willesden Green: 'May contain nuts.'

❖

MAJOR TITLES 2001

The 1000 Guineas
Dr G. Garden (Fowl presented by Bedford Matthews)

Roll of Honour
East Ham & Cheese

International Croix de Gare
Victor Hugo (Paris Metro)

Leytonstone Formula I Grand Prix
Herne Hill (Damon's younger brother)

The Berlei Doubles Cup
Denise van Often

Palmer-Tomkinson Plate
(Unclaimed)

Cup Winners' Saucer
Hammersmith Academicals

6 Stations Crown
Wales (1st year running)

The Dante Gabriel Rosette
John Everett Mill-Hill & Holborn Hunt

Flower Arrangement in an Egg-cup
Timothy Brook-Taylor (Again!)

Best of Breed
B. Cryer (Wind-assisted)

General Knowledge Hat
H. Lyttelton (6Q)

Armitage Shanks Charity Bowl (Presented to the winner of the UK Domestic League grand final)
C. Sell. Winning score: 1, declared

THE MORNINGTON CRESCENT ACADEMY AWARDS

Best Move
From Here to East Tilbury (Upset of the season)

Best Make-up
L'Uton

Best Musical
Grays and Dollis (Hill)

Best Move in a Foreign Language
Crouch End Tiger, Hendon Dragon

THE STOVOLD MEMORIAL LECTURE
18 February 2001

Delivered by Sir M.T. Cresshunt
At the Convention Room (annexe E),
Stovoldotel Continental, Fiddlers Hamlet.
(Off exit 26 M25, nearest tube: Theydon Bois)

My Lord Topmost Worshipful Griffon of the Line, Arcane Officers of the Supreme, Ancient, and Hallowed Order of Tubers, Grand Masters, Masters, Mistresses and Wives; Crescenteers, Crescentettes, Morningteens, Morningtots, and friends of the Crescent. It gives me great pleasure...and it has done for many years! Ha Ha Ha! (Thanks Barry!) *(Restless murmurs, discreet calls for more wine, etc.)*

It is an honour and a pleasure for me, in my capacity as Gold Ticket Punch Pursuivant and Fixed Penalty, to deliver this keynote memorial address to you all here tonight. *(Muttering and whispers of 'What?')*

My subject this evening is a topic that concerns us all, every single one of us, day in and night out. It is quite simply 'The State of the Game at the start of the 21st century'. Indeed I believe I can say, without fear of contradiction... *(Heckler: 'No you can't!')*...I believe I can say that the Great Game goes from strength to strength. As I travel about the world in my capacity as Chairman of Stovold.dot.co.dot.uk.dot.co.dot.ltd, I get it again and again from many different lips, which is always a source of much pleasure to me.

Could we have the first slide please?

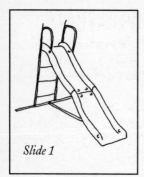

Slide 1

Many of you will recognise the popular Stovoldkid Avalanche Playslide, available from all retail outlets, and one of our best-sellers. But not even the popularity of a top-class piece of executive-style leisure merchandise in three sizes can match the abiding, nay *growing* appeal of our Glorious Game.*(Laughter and comments)*

But now I move, if I may, from witticism to criticism. Yes, we are all aware that our beloved MCC is not above reproach. I refer, as you have no doubt already surmised, to the vexed question of Lady Members. For nigh on 250 years we have grappled with this knotty problem, and one would have thought that, at the dawn of the 21st century, we would have resolved it. But no, the women are still with us, and we can't get them out. *(Hail of cutlery)*

Please yourselves. On a lighter note, let us now turn to the obituary list of stalwart members who have boarded that long escalator from this mortal coil to the great Game in the sky. Let us hold in our thoughts the names of 'Bufty' Wilberforce, 'Tufty' Spinks, Nigel Copstock, and 'Mufty' Charteris, who have drawn up a list of the deceased members, which can be seen sellotaped to the side of the soft drinks dispenser by the fire exit.

Well I can see the Loughborough Junction Jumbo Jills are lining up to delight us with their display of Synchronised Slimming, so I shall conclude by drawing your attention to the reverse of your menus where you will find application forms for the Stovoldcon Mornington Crescent Room-style Accomodation Time-Share Flat-you-lent scheme. Thank you, and long live the Game! *(Sits to loud cheers and applause (taped))*

NATIONAL CHAMPIONSHIPS
Updated list of all winners of the Mornington Crescent
National Champion Trophy Shield. 1720–1880

1720 Sir Edwin 'South Sea' Bubble
A very unsteady and uninspired player, and an
unpopular champion, nevertheless a very private person.
Qualifying scores: 1–0, 1–0, 1–0, 1–0, 0–1, 0–1, 1–0, 1–0.

1740 Jem Doenitz
A steady rather than an inspired player, this somewhat
mysterious figure was often cited as steady rather than
inspired, nevertheless a very private person. (Controversially,
he married 'Tough' Nell Park, one of the few women
amateurs to have a Tube Station named like her.)
Qualifying scores: 1–0, 1–0, 1–0, 1–0, 0–1, 0–1, 1–0, 1–0.

1760 N.F. Stovold
A steady rather than an inspired player, a popular
champion, first introduced to the game at school, then
working through the minor and county leagues before
achieving international status. Author of *The Origin
and Rules*, and Founder of the MCC in 1780, he
launched the first Almanac in 1782. His colourful
association with the Game is detailed in his biography
On the Game by Humphrey Carpenders-Park. Often
cited as one of the Game's most meticulous, nit-picking,
unyielding, short, and popular founding fathers,
nevertheless a very private person.
Qualifying scores: 1–0, 1–0, 1–0, 1–0, 0–1, 0–1, 1–0, 1–0.

1780 Lady Georgina Watts-Watt
(First MCC champion)

A steady rather than an inspired player, Lady Georgina raised eyebrows wherever she went. In fact she could raise them both together or one at a time – just one of the many party

tricks for which she was justly famed. A popular and much loved champion, she was a noted eccentric who favoured male clothing and involved herself in robust pursuits, many of which ended in her capture. Always inventive in her play, she explored a wide range of openings. Often cited as one of the Game's most voracious, predatory, disturbing, overpowering, boisterous, and frightening figures, nevertheless a very private person.

Qualifying scores: 1–0, 1–0, 1–0, 1–0, 0–1, 0–1, 1–0, 1–0.

1800 Sir Evelyn Watts-Watt

A steady rather than an inspired player, the first and only National Champion to *inherit* the title. In a controversial play-off against William Blake to decide the championship, Watts-Watt surprisingly won by a Wapping Clapham and Turnham Green manoeuvre. To show there were no hard feelings, Blake painted an exceedingly ugly portrait of Sir Evelyn, which was none the less flattering. Not unnaturally, he was a very private person.

Qualifying scores: 1–0, 1–0, 1–0, 1–0, 0–1, 0–1, 1–0, 1–0.

1820 Adam 'Trouble' Adams

A steady rather than an inspired player, this colourful character tried his hand at a number of trades – lumberjack, costermonger, hatter, lumbermonger, and natterjack – before settling down as a midwife. Often cited as one of the Game's most footloose and feckless characters, nevertheless a very private person.

Qualifying scores: 1–0, 1–0, 1–0, 1–0, 0–1, 0–1, 1–0, 1–0.

1840 Sir Eric Threepin-Plugg

A *very* private person.

Qualifying scores: 1–0, 1–0, 1–0, 1–0, 0–1, 0–1, 1–0, 1–0.

1860 'Little' Sid Boophus

A steady rather than an inspired player, this 'popular' Music Hall Artiste – 'The Infant Juggler' – proved to be an irritating champion. Often cited as one of the Game's most aggravating, conceited, cruel, and least funny competitors, nevertheless a very private person.

Qualifying scores: 1–0, 1–0, 1–0, 1–0, 0–1, 0–1, 1–0, 1–0.

1880 Dr W.G. Grace

A steady rather than an inspired player, Mornington Crescent was very much his second sport, his greatest triumphs being in the field of Cross-country Badminton. Many amusing stories are told of his eccentricity and genius. On one famous occasion, during a crucial regional final at Arnos Grove, he did nothing amusing at all! Often cited as one of the Game's most eccentric, gifted and popular players, nevertheless a very private person.

Qualifying scores: 1–0, 1–0, 1–0, 1–0, 0–1, 0–1, 1–0, 1–0.

SNACKS AND PICNICS
For the Great Outdoors

Nothing beats the fun of eating in the open air – or *'al fiasco'* as the French have it. On the beach, on the patio, in the lay-by, or on the Underground, there's a special thrill in opening the hamper and seeing what falls out into the dirt. However, many Crescenteers on their travels have tired of the same old menu of hard-boiled veg, a ham and cheese Club biscuit, or a fruit. Celebrity Chef Jamie Oliverpool-Street has produced some novel ideas for the picnic table, as well as offering some old ways with new favourites. *'Bona Petit!'*

BARBICAN SPARE RIBS

An outdoor barbican is always great fun! You can build your own camp fire out of whatever you find lying around the countryside – straw, twigs, brushwood, outbuildings, sheep, and so on – or you can do it the professional way with a Stovold Scorcher Mk III (available by Mail Order, including licence). At the end of the day, most butchers will have a few left-over ribs going cheap, and they will also have plenty of offal they will be happy for you to take off their hands – so bring a scraping tool and a damp cloth to help you remove it.

Ingredients

1 clutch of pig ribs
a selection of recovered offal
1 clove of hoof
1 can of Smoky Pete's Hickory Polyurethane Glazing Varnish

Method
Cook the ribs
Extinguish the fire if possible
Serve and run

KENSAL RICE

A savoury rice dish, delicious served on its own, or fairly edible as an accompaniment to Bacon-Tree, Heron Quiche, or Bangers-and-Amersham. Best prepared the day before, and left at home.

Ingredients

6 kilos of long play rice
1 metric cupful of stock
1 metric pint of Thai-dyed prawns
4 sun-dried potatoes
1 metric handful of chopped cream
1 medium chive, skinned and jointed
1 metric pinch of sea salt (or sea pepper if preferred)
1 knob of mustard

Method
Boil rice (20 minutes per leg)
Stir in the aubergine paste and greengage purée
Arrange the Whelk Segments around the Melon Ball
Bring the Dripping to the boil and drizzle all over
Wipe up carefully before serving

BAKER'S TREAT

Nothing spoils an outdoor feast in the countryside more than a sudden downpour of rain, or of anything else. This dish forms a tasty and practical addition to any picnic basket. Created by Celebrity Chef Marco

Pierre-Whitechapel, this ingenious recipe won its inventor a coveted Michelin Tyre in 1987.

Ingredients

24 pitta breads
17 metres of spaghetti (cooked)
1 long French loaf

Method

Stitch the pittas together, using the spaghetti, to form a disc about 3 metric feet in diameter. Nail the French loaf to the centre of the disc. Now you simply hold your Baker's Treat over your head like a large mushroom, and you and your picnic guests will be as dry as a bone. But remember, if it rains the bread will immediately become soaking wet and floppy, so it is a good idea to keep it dry under an umbrella, or large mushroom.

PICCALILLI CIRCUS

Every child remembers seeing the Clowns on that first visit to the Circus. Ask any therapist. So here's a fun way to serve pickles at an outdoor kiddies' party. Just wait till you see their little faces!

Ingredients

1 jar of Piccalilli mustard pickle
1 large cabbage leaf (raw)
Brazil nuts (whole)
tomato ketchup
1 ripe Stilton cheese
1 large boned chicken (you could just ask for a 'fat' chicken, but 'large-boned' is kinder)

Method

Set out the pickles on the uncooked chicken to form a Clown face: pickled onions for eyes, gherkin for nose, cauliflower lumps for ears, miscellaneous bits for warts etc. Arrange the Brazil nuts to represent sharp, irregular, stained teeth, and smear the ripe Stilton all over to give the disturbing appearance of unhealthy skin, and to create the authentic 'Clowny' smell of the Circus. Splash liberally with ketchup, especially around the mouth and eyes. Cover with the cabbage leaf, then at the last minute remove the leaf and hear the little ones scream! (Can be frozen and used over and over again!)

TULSE EEL

'Ere's a right old Cockerney favourite and no mistake, I should coco! Gor Streuth, Gor Blimey, Gor Vidal, Missus! Blowed if this ain't a slap-up nosh fit for a toff, Lor' luvaduck or what?! If you're tired of the old Jellied Eels, i.e. after the second mouthful (only jokin' me old Muckers!), then here's a tasty alternative – Eels in Blancmange.

Ingredients

1 gallon of eels (optional)
apples and pears
rabbit
frog and toad
1 well beaten egg
1 badly mashed potato
1 sachet of Stovoldfare Blancmange Mix
add salt and pepper to taste (hold nose not to taste)

Method

Once you have killed, skinned and gutted the eels, cut

them into chunks and sear the pieces in an eeling skillet. Leave the heads on for effect. Bring all the ingredients to the boil, after adding whatever water you can find nearby. Simmer gently while waiting for it to cook, then take a deep breath and take it off the heat. Slap it on the Old China and tuck in!

SWISS COTTAGE PIE

An Alpine favourite, this traditional dish comes from the Cuckoo Farmers of the Clocktanzenspielglocken Canton in the Dutch Alps. Colourful fare, easy-to-do, and an economical way to use up those unsightly left-overs.

Ingredients

pie crust

pie filling

Method

Day 1 – cook, but do not eat

Day 2 – eat left-overs

PUDDINGTON

Time for afters, yippee! Forget tiramisu, forget profiteroles, forget strawberry tarte tatin! Forget them all, because you haven't got them. You've got Puddington.

Ingredients

1 large organically reared suet

3 bushels (or grams) self-raising flour

1 self-flouring raisin

18 dried apricot quarters

double cream (or 2 single creams)

1 dessicated coconut

2 pinches of barking powder

3–4 handfuls of treacle

Method

Stir the ingredients together and mould the mixture into the shape of a pudding. Tie up in a muslin cloth and steam in a Travelling Oven or kiln at 450°C for 24 hours. Serve with tiramisu, profiteroles, or strawberry tarte tatin.

AFTER PINNER MINTS

What better way to round off a square meal than a beaker of warm coffee and a refreshing sweetmeat? If you are taking your picnic on the Metropolitan Line westbound, you will find you are ready for your beverage as you approach Moor Park – hence the name of this delicacy.

Ingredients

360 grams of finest quality beef or lamb mints

12 pecks of icing sugar (pasteurised)

half a family-sized egg

1 slab of industrial chocolate

Method

Mix the mints, icing sugar, and egg to a smooth paste, and fry till crisp. Warm the chocolate until it is soft, then mould it by hand into 12 to 84 polyhedral cases. Pour the mints filling into the cases, and staple them shut. Cool in the refrigerator, isn't it? Serve on a bed of lemon grass.

SMIRKEY'S GAME
By John le Cabbé

The house was set well back from the corner of Headstone Lane. A thin sleety rain drifted through the bitter night air, and the crumbling once-grand façade glistened in the jaundiced glow of a street-lamp. George Smirkey crunched his way up the short driveway then, throwing aside the empty crisp packet, he mounted the three worn stone steps and rapped on the doorbell. The door was cautiously opened almost at once by a man of middle age with receding grey hair, a nervous moustache, and a world-weary pair of spectacles on his face.

'Is this the "Safe" house?' asked Smirkey.

'It is,' replied Mr Safe. 'What can I do for you?'

'I am a Jehovah's Witness,' responded Smirkey, dutifully giving the password the 'Circus Operators' had provided him with before he set out from MI7 (SIC/WD40) HQ at Finchley Central.

'Then you'd better come in from the cold,' said Safe, sighing as he stepped back to allow his visitor to enter. Smirkey slipped past his host into the hallway. Struggling to his feet, he noticed the two men in dark suits and heavily framed spectacles who were sitting on the bench by the phone. One of them opened his briefcase smartly and approached Smirkey, holding out a document.

'Might I interest you in a copy of *The Watch Tower*?' he asked, with a wolfish grin. George Smirkey turned to Safe and raised a quizzical eyelid. Safe shrugged dismissively.

'They gave the password,' he explained.

'Get rid of them,' said Smirkey softly, tying a knot in his mental handkerchief to remind him to memo the 'Circus Operators' telling them to brush up their act. Not only did their juggling with fiery rings leave much to be desired, but their recent password selections had become decidedly shoddy: 'I'm a little teapot, short and stout' and 'You up for it, big boy?' had been two of their latest embarrassments. As Mr Safe ushered the two men of God out of the front door, Smirkey looked round. Not fat exactly, but verging on the spherical.

'Where's the Special Delivery?' he asked.

'Top of the stairs,' said Safe, closing the door, 'second on the right. You have to pull the chain twice.'

'No,' said Smirkey with weary patience, 'the Special Delivery, the Package.' Safe stared at him blankly. 'The Item? The You-know-what? The bloke, for God's sake! The *bloke!*'

'Oh, *that* bloke, the Parcel, him!' exclaimed Safe. 'Yes, he's top of the stairs, second on the right. Been there two hours or more. Remind him about the chain, would you?'

Smirkey grunted as Safe shuffled off to the back kitchen. As he disappeared from sight his slippers squeaked annoyingly on the thin linoleum, so Smirkey kicked them back under the bench, which soon shut them up. Then he climbed the narrow stairway.

At the top of the stairs Smirkey stared at the flimsy wooden door covered in cheap brown varnish. He couldn't see who had thrown the varnish at him, but as he rubbed the worst of it off his overcoat with a handkerchief, he thought he heard a low chuckle from an open doorway at the end of the landing. Smirkey approached the doorway silently then, standing to one side, he pushed his bowler hat on the end of his umbrella across the opening, into the eyeline of whoever was inside the room.

'God, you've lost weight,' drawled a voice from within. 'Well come on in George, I've been waiting for you.'

Across the shabby room a languid figure lay propped up on one arm on the bed. Nicholas 'Fag' Stanford-le-Hope gestured vaguely to a bentwood chair. Smirkey sat down. Stanford-le-Hope gestured to the chair more specifically, and Smirkey rose from the floor and sat on the chair. On the table at his elbow stood an almost full bottle of varnish remover and a rag. As he dabbed at the worst of the stains, Smirkey regarded the man opposite. Though clearly on his uppers (a half-empty pill bottle lay on the blanket) there was still about him an air of faded elegance, of class. The suit, though threadbare and crumpled, had Savile Row stamped all over it – an economical purchase following some promotional campaign. The scuffed brogues were well made, and dyed that exclusive Geography Master Orange favoured by the upper classes. The club tie marked him out as a Crescenteer, First Class, and in spite of his reduced circumstances, he still sported a colourful Kleenex in his breast pocket. Smirkey had not seen him for years, but the superior air of the man was still intact.

Stanford-le-Hope was educated at Harrow, then after a series of business failures, found himself a job as a travelling salesman with Thomson and Morganton, Horticultural Suppliers. He was a typical ex-public school boy gone to seed. Smirkey had first seen him at Upton Park Garden Centre, and had at once identified him as potential MI7 material. Indeed he had turned him there and then.

'Get off!' Stanford-le-Hope had shouted, breaking free. Smirkey had calmed him, and by way of reassurance had told him all about Finchley Central and its activities, its personnel, the names of its field agents, and details of all its current operations. Snapping shut his notebook, putting away his pencil, and turning off his pocket tape recorder, the young man had agreed at once to become one of Smirkey's people. His first venture in the field had been when he was dropped into the Ukraine, and he was transmitting back to base before he hit the ground. His first requisition was for a parachute.

Now Stanford-le-Hope was back, and the 'De-Baggers' at Finchley Central had sent Smirkey to persuade him to give up the information he was known to hold. The man on the bed smiled, adjusting his twin monocles.

'It's Leon "C",' he grinned, 'he's coming over.'

Leon 'C'. The Head of Moscow Central at Nevsky Prospect. Of course rumours had reached the ears of the 'Curtain-Twitchers' at GCHQ Chesham, but this was the final confirmation that MI7 had been waiting for.

'Yes,' drawled Stanford-le-Hope, 'he left his dacha on Sunday night in a horse-drawn babushka with the blinds drawn. Then from Nevsky Prospect he was driven in a Mug limousine to Gorky Park, and there he went underground. Berlin, Paris, Bounds Green, Turnpike Lane, Caledonian Road...'

'He's...here?' gasped Smirkey.

'Waiting to see you,' murmured Stanford-le-Hope.

'Where?'

'The Underground Car Park, obviously.'

'Of course!'

Leon 'C' was an old Moscow hand, and would naturally follow tradition.

'What I need now is a Safe Drop,' said Smirkey, rising and scratching his head on a light bracket.

'It's only a couple of feet down to the shed roof,' said Stanford-le-Hope, indicating the half-open window.

'Sounds safe enough to me,' said Smirkey, wasting no time in struggling through the opening. 'Thanks.'

Moments later, having torn his coat pocket on the window latch, he was on the roof of the shed. The corrugated tin was slick with rain, and he lost his footing, skidding heavily down the slope. He somersaulted twice, bending his umbrella and jamming his bowler hat firmly over his eyes. He reached out wildly to grab at a piano which had been thoughtlessly dumped up there, but the precarious instrument toppled over and went tumbling down, flinging him over the edge to land bottom first in a rain barrel which exploded under his weight in a cascade of stale water. The small torrent swept Smirkey across the path, depositing him in a newly manured plot of laurel and hardy annuals. Smirkey struggled to his feet fuming, and steaming a bit after the drenching. To vent his annoyance he kicked out at a cat, but missed, which only infuriated him further, as it had taken him the best part of twenty minutes to find one.

Smirkey found his car where he had left it – at home in the garage – and drove off into the night. Leon 'C' was waiting for him somewhere in an Underground Car Park. He knew which one.

❖

The Underground Car Park at Goodge Street had been built in the 1970s by MI7 as a specially designated location for clandestine meetings. Unfortunately members of the public kept parking their cars there, and strangers were forever blundering into important secret negotiations, so Finchley Central closed it down. It remained empty and unused until the late 1980s, when some bright spark at Belsize Park sub-HQ (NW) pointed out that an empty and unused Underground Car Park would be a perfect location for clandestine meetings. The Committee for Clandestine Meeting Arrangements (the 'Matchmakers') took this brilliant idea on board and acted on it at once, so in early 1991 a brand new empty and unused Underground Car Park was built at Mornington Crescent as a specially designated location for clandestine meetings. That was where Smirkey was heading.

Once inside the Car Park, Smirkey switched off the engine and peered into the silent gloom between the long rows of concrete pillars. A distant figure emerged from the shadows, and rapidly approached the car.

'You can't park here,' boomed the uniformed attendant, wagging an admonitory clipboard, 'we are empty and unused. Be off with you!'

'I'm here for a meeting,' said Smirkey, flourishing his ID badge for the man to read.

'Sorry, Mr Smokey, your name isn't on the docket,' said the attendant, scanning his empty clipboard.

'Do you know the meaning of Class A clearance?' growled the spymaster, growing exasperated.

'Class A Clearance? Oh, that's different. Well it's different from Class B Clearance, isn't it?'

'I have Class A Clearance, I have a meeting, and I have Finchley Central Authority. Right?'

'Fair enough, guv. Carry on.'

'Thank you.'

'Don't mention it. But you can't park here.'

'Why not? This is a bloody Car Park!'

'Yes,' explained the attendant, as if to a tiny child, 'but it is empty, and it is unused.'

'It is not empty, because my car is in it, and therefore it is far from unused. Savvy?'

'How did you know my name?' asked 'Savvy' Saveloy the attendant, reeling under Smirkey's intellectual onslaught. 'It's a rare thing nowadays, the personal touch,' he went on. 'I don't see many folk down here, me. Well not since 1991 when the builders left. Yes, it's a lonely old life underground. Makes a pleasant change to see a kindly face, have a bit of a chat. Going anywhere nice for your holidays?'

Suddenly Smirkey was alerted by some uncanny sixth sense. Perhaps it was a seventh sense. Perhaps it wasn't a sense at all. Whatever it was, it alerted him. They were not alone…

'They tell me Magalouf can be quite a lively spot,' said Savvy, wistfully.

Smirkey whirled round. When he stopped whirling, he saw a tall muscular figure standing before him in a bulky fur hat. Stepping out of the hat, the figure approached silently and walked into the light. There was a muffled oath, and a clatter as the light fell over, then, rubbing his temple where he had caught it, the stranger came face to face with Smirkey. The two men regarded each other for a long moment.

'At last,' whispered the stranger.

'Leon,' said Smirkey.

The men looked into each other's eyes in silence.

'Either of you gents see the match on Saturday?'

enquired Savvy.

Ignoring him, the two men who had never met, yet who knew each other so intimately well, shook hands.

'So good to see you at last, Smudger,' said Leon 'C' warmly.

'You too, Chalky,' said George 'Smudger' Smirkey.

'So much has changed,' mused Leon 'Chalky' 'C', 'now that the Cold War is over.'

'Is it?' said Smirkey, a knowing half-smile playing about his lips.

'Yes.'

'What, honestly?' said Smirkey, his face falling. 'I hadn't heard.'

'Oh yes. There's no place now for old dinosaurs like you and me. That's why I came over. The job prospects here are much better than in Moscow. I plan to return to the old trade I followed before my days at Nevsky Prospect.'

'What old trade was that?'

'I was a boot-maker. I plan to find work in a branch of your chain of high street boot emporiums.'

'Chain?' said Smirkey, puzzled, 'what chain?'

'They call themselves simply "Boots",' said Leon, letting out a roar of laughter. 'How typically English and straightforward!' he guffawed. Now it was Smirkey's turn to let out a roar of laughter.

'How typically Soviet and naive,' he guffawed in turn. 'Didn't you realise they are a cover? They have nothing to do with boot-makers!'

Leon's brow darkened.

'They're chemist's shops, guv,' explained Savvy, adjusting the lamp to brighten the Russian's brow.

'Well,' said Leon, perching himself thoughtfully on an upturned pigeon, 'perhaps they will still give me a job.

Maybe you might even join me.'

'Yes. Yes you go to work for the Pharmaceutical Companies if you must,' spat Smirkey, 'if you can stomach their ruthless commercialism, their immoral exploitation of the sick and needy, their cynical profiteering from the suffering of others and their heartless contempt for the Third World. Sorry. Bit of a hobby horse.'

'I'm sure I can overcome any scruples,' replied Leon with a smile. 'Perhaps you might even join me.'

'What's the money like?' said Smirkey.

A voice came from the darkness. It rang around the bare concrete walls like a whiplash.

'It seems I got here just in time,' said a shadowy figure, walking into the light. 'Ouch!'

'Sorry, I should have moved it,' said Savvy. 'Still raining out, is it?'

Smirkey looked up with dismay at the new arrival. It was none other that Alan 'Stella' Rickmansworth, Overall Controller of MI7, Finchley Central.

'Sod off Stella,' barked Smirkey, 'we don't need any bloody overalls.'

'How you can say that I do not know!' exclaimed Stella. 'Look at the state of you. Is that brown varnish?'

Smirkey sheepishly took the crisp white overall Stella held out to him, and began struggling into it.

'And a nice bright red one for you, Mr "C",' said the overall supervisor, handing the defecting Russian a neatly shrinkwrapped package. 'They're sticklers for colour-coding at Finchley Central. Anyway it'll go nicely with your bootees.'

A single shot rang out, the echoes clattering around the dark spaces like ball bearings in a kettle. Smirkey, Leon, and Stella dived for cover behind a concrete column.

'Is that Olympia Dukakis still going?' wondered Savvy, unaware of the neat round hole that was still smoking in the centre of his clipboard. Nicholas 'Fag' Stanford-le-Hope stepped out of the shadows, neatly sidestepped the light, and approached the cowering figures. A Totteridge & Whetstone .38 semi-automatic nestled in his hand. A contemptuous smile hovered around his face. He swatted it away like a moth.

'I'll make a brew, shall I?' called Savvy from his booth to which he had retreated. 'Hello!' he exclaimed, 'who's been putting ball bearings in my kettle?'

The trio behind the column had all drawn their weapons.

'Drop the gun, Nicholas,' called Smirkey, 'I've known for some time that you were a double agent.'

'I knew that too,' said Leon 'C'.

'Well I suspected it myself when he put in a requisition for two pairs of overalls,' hissed Stella.

'Look around,' said Stanford-le-Hope, 'you're surrounded. Throw down your weapons.'

The three cowering agents looked around and saw uniformed figures advancing towards them. Their position was hopeless. They threw out their guns and knives, knuckledusters, catapults, and books on karate.

'I knew you'd see sense,' purred the traitor. 'And just to show there are no hard feelings, I'm prepared to offer you all a job.'

'Work for you?' sneered Smirkey. 'Who's been running you, Nicholas? CIA? KGB?'

'NCP. Interested?'

'What's the money like?' asked Smirkey.

❖

ANNUAL RULE CHANGES
2001 Season

Changes to Stovold's Rules of the Game, as agreed at the Annual Peculiar Meeting of the Rule-Changing Committee with special responsibility for Changing Rules and Miscellaneous Amendments to the Laws of the Game, with particular reference to Changes in the Rules (of the Game).

RULE 147.22a Angle of the Diagonal.

'The Angle of the Diagonal is to be no less than 45 degrees and no greater than 53 degrees within the Perimeter Boundings.' (Warburton's 'new' modification, adopted in 1923)

Note that some players, especially when engaged in the Contract or Auction versions of the game, still prefer to use Old Stovold's Original Ruling:

'The Angle of the Diagonal is 48 degrees, and that's all there is to it.'

After much deliberation, and frequent reference to *Archbold's Logarithmic Metropolitan Progressions*, the Committee has agreed to ratify these rulings, the new simplified wording to be adopted being:

'The Angle of the Diagonal (hereinafter 'the angle') shall be agreed to be any angle being agreed to be an angle agreed to be between the angles of 1 degree and the angle of 359 degrees Celsius.'

(As before, the Rule does not apply if one or more players are holding Tadge.)

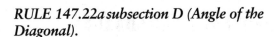

RULE 147.22a subsection D (*Angle of the Diagonal*).

In response to the deluge of queries we have received from Mrs Trellis of North Wales in her letter, the clarification of subsection D of this Rule would seem to be required. The first part of this subsection deals with the definition of **Diagonal** as used in normal play during the Classic and Modern Game.

The **Diagonal** is deemed to be that line which is not **Monagonal**, and is therefore one part removed from the linear conjunction of notified Stations or Blots. This also applies to **Polyagonal**, **Hemiagonal**, and **Anagonal** lines in all circumstances barring Nip. Monangular Triangles and Acute Ellipsoid Trajectories are not affected.

A   C, or N

A Diagonal laid out flat for clarity

NB – it is important to distinguish between the **Diagonal** and the **Oblique**. Although they may appear be interchangeable, as indeed they usually are, they serve very different purposes when Helwett's Proscription is in force, or when the Game is played under Floodlights. The **Ob-lique**, being the natural opposite of the **Lique**, is therefore not related to the **Monagonal** line in the same way that the **Diagonal** is, especially in the purlieu of, say, Kensington Olympia or Uxbridge. Players trapped in **Diagony**, however, may well find themselves in need of a **Lique**.

A   C, T, or S

An Oblique straightened out for clarity.

RULE 94.13c Above and Below the Line.

'A Location or Property is either above the Line or it isn't.' (Old Stovold's Original Line Law)

This law was modified by the Minogue Commission in 1954 as follows:
'A Location or Property is either above the Line or it is not.'

Confusion has long reigned over the strict interpretation of this law. The situation was not improved by the schism of 1977, which saw the World Wide Mornington Crescent Federation (WWMCF) break away from the previously unchallenged authority of the World Wide Mornington Crescent Association (WWMCA), under the aegis of Don Casta-Rovas. In effect this has led to the existence of two separate Leagues, competing for two separate sets of Championship Belts, Rose Bowls, Cups, Saucers, and Spoons. In an attempt at conciliation between the WWMCF (Old Stovold's Original) and the WWMCA (Minogue Modification), the committee puts forward the following clarification, in the hope that the two authorities will agree to combine to form a Super-League under the aegis of the Don:

'Insofar as it is hereinafter agreed that there is a line above or below which any property or location may be agreed to be deemed to be then those agreed to be above the line shall be deemed to be above the line and those properties or locations deemed to be agreed to be below the line shall be agreed to be accepted as being deemed to be below the line and not as in the converse case that is deemed to be above the agreed line.' (This is offered as a guideline only, and not as a binding regulation at this, or any other time.)

RULE 226.16c–27h   Crabbit's Law.

'The illegality of vectored access to low coordinates within the Rhombus of Apperley is non-negotiable under any circumference.' (Crabbit's Law, part IIa)

This sweeping statement no longer applies, following the adoption of Quantum play. Crabbit's Law per se naturally remains in force, but players are now allowed to ignore all sections from 16c to 27h, except one.

Caricature of Humphrey Crabbit, emphasising his dainty feet and uncommonly large head.

RULE 159347.1a   Correct Forms of Address.

'Correct Forms of Address must be used to all Club Officers and Visiting Dignitaries.' (Gallagher's Appendix: Etiquette)

It being felt that some of the language enshrined in the traditional greetings and eulogies appears quaint and risible in this day and age, the following changes to the form of words are suggested:

Substitute:	Welcome for All Hail, Distinguished for Most Adored, and Colleague for Muffin.
Remove:	Helmet, Cloak, Sword, Sash, Pantaloons.
Then insert:	Umbrella.

FAIRLOP'S LAST THEOREM

In 1637, the brilliant French Numberographologist, Professeur Pierre de Fairlop, was visiting London to show off. He stayed briefly with the academic and wit, Sir Timothy Broke-Tailleur (Captain of Berks). In a vain attempt to entertain the Frenchman, Sir Tim beguiled him with an explanation of Hugo's Parabola, which includes the mysteriously unprovable equation:

$$\text{Leicester}^2 + \text{Sloane}^2 = \text{Trafalgar}^2$$

(Which does not apply for *any Square north of Leicester*!)

Next morning at breakfast, the cocky Frenchman announced that he had worked out the answer, and hastily scribbled the proof in the margarine. Broke-Tailleur was amazed, and as Fairlop hurried off to catch his Last Tram, the brilliant Captain of Berks mulled over the astounding discovery as he washed up the dishes. Till his dying day, Sir Timothy regretted wiping down the margarine dish, as a result of which Fairlop's miraculous proof was lost for ever, never to be seen again. Or so it was thought...

300 years later the gifted Cambridge Mathematopian C.T. Thameslink became intrigued by the famous conundrum, and set out to recreate Fairlop's solution. After years of diligent calculation and research, including the exploration of several blind alleys (in one of which he was stopped and cautioned by the police), Thameslink found himself on the brink of the breakthrough he was seeking. At last, using Poke's differential, quantum trigonometry, chaos theory, and the very finest margarine, the Cambridge genius announced his discovery to the world.

Thameslink described his equation as 'of enormous importance to the world of Mathematics, and of the greatest value to all players of the Great Game.' Sadly he was wrong on both points.

OLD STOVOLD'S PUZZLE PAGE!

No MCC *Almanac* would be complete without its Puzzle Page, as a gesture to those few fans of Mornington Crescent who actually enjoy playing games. Here is this year's jolly selection for your attention.

HIDDEN DESTINATIONS!

In the square below you'll find there are any number of hidden destinations. They may be read across, right to left or left to right, or up or down, or even on the diagonal! No looping, but see how many you can find anyway!

M	Q	O	P	A	R	M	U	N	W
Z	O	I	S	L	K	N	F	O	K
O	C	R	E	S	C	E	N	T	E
L	J	I	N	C	D	S	S	U	P
B	C	D	F	I	L	G	H	J	K
L	V	M	O	W	N	X	P	Y	Q
R	Z	S	B	T	C	G	D	V	F
W	G	X	A	H	Z	B	T	C	J
D	K	F	A	G	L	I	H	O	J
K	M	L	B	M	C	N	D	F	N

WHICH LINE IS LONGEST?
An optical illusion

Northern Line

─────────────────────────

─────────────────────────

Central Line

MCC NATIONAL CHAMPIONSHIPS
Updated list of all winners of the Mornington
Crescent Club National Champion Trophy Shield. 1900–2001

1900 Humphrey 'Humph' Lyttelton

A steady rather than an inspired player and popular champion, first introduced to the Game at Eton School for the Sons of Parents, he refined his game during service in the Right Guards (where he took part in several daring underarm-cover missions), before working through the minor and county leagues and at last achieving international status. A Grand Master since 1957, he once played a simultaneous Game against 32 ranked County Players at the same time, and lost heavily. Since then he has concentrated on his career as a Class A Umpire, where his powers of intense concentration, penetrating analysis, and swift decisiveness have yet to become obvious. Often cited as one of the Game's most rambunctious, boisterous and loud trumpet players, nevertheless a very private person.
Qualifying scores: 1–0, 1–0, 1–0, 1–0, 0–1, 0–1, 1–0, 1–0.

1920 Arthur 'Boy' Allbright

A steady rather than an inspired player, this popular society figure owned a Night Club, which he kept for self-defence. He is best remembered for 'Allbright's Opening', a gambit which he amazingly devised the *very first time* he played the Game. When asked if he knew any good first moves, he replied 'Vauxhall!' and so a legend was born. Often cited as one of the Game's most sociable, dim, and inebriated men-about-town, nevertheless a very private person.
Qualifying scores: 1–0, 1–0, 1–0, 1–0, 0–1, 0–1, 1–0, 1–0.

1940 'Tinker' Beaumont VC

A steady rather than an inspired player, he picked up the Game in a POW camp where he was held by the Germans from 1919 to 1939 'just in case'. After escaping and volunteering to join the Navy, he became one of the original 'Cockleshell Heroes' when he commanded a one-man midget Aircraft Carrier which he sailed into enemy waters under cover of dampness, and single-handedly sank. For this action he was awarded the Victoria Crescent. Often cited as one of the Game's most attractive, daring and moist players, nevertheless a very private person.

Qualifying scores: 1–0, 1–0, 1–0, 1–0, 0–1, 0–1, 1–0, 1–0.

1960 Zappa 'Moon Petal' Tripp

A steady rather than an inspired player, this humble Crust Technician at the Mothers Pride Bakery became a leading light in the Flour Power movement. He was famously photographed stuffing a baguette down a rifle barrel outside the American Embassy. A popular champion, first introduced to the joys of Crescenteering in the Detention Camp, he is still often cited as one of the Game's most laid-back, colourful, sad, and unhygienic players, nevertheless a very private person.

Qualifying scores: 1–0, 1–0, 1–0, 1–0, 0–1, 0–1, 1–0, 1–0.

1980 L/Cpl Tommy 'Goose' Green

A steady rather than an inspired player, a popular champion, first introduced to the Game while recovering from a penguin bite. The Lance Corporal brought a soldier's eye to the Game, which he insisted on showing around to the rest of the competitors before the match, invariably putting them off their stride. Often cited as one of the Game's most aggressive, jingoistic, mercenary and antisocial players, nevertheless a very private person.

Qualifying scores: 1–0, 1–0, 1–0, 1–0, 0–1, 0–1, 1–0, 1–0.

2000 Gryigoryi Efyimovyich Ryudyetskyi

A steady rather than an inspired player, this 'Man of Kent' soon became the darling of the circuit. Son of a peasant girl and a Balalaika Repair Man from Syandvitch, the youngster showed early promise, and after his National Championship triumph became a firm favourite with the ladies, who thought of him as a Hot Tip. Indeed, the whole country was rooting for him when it looked as if we might at last have a home-grown British World Champion. Unhappily, just before the International Finals, a nagging skin condition forced him to scratch.

Still regarded as a great hope for the future, against all the evidence, 'Gryig' is still cited as one of the Game's most heavily-accented, plucky and popular players, but is nevertheless a very private person.

Qualifying scores: 1–0, 1–0, 1–0, 1–0, 0–1, 0–1, 1–0, 1–0.

❖

SENIOR MEMBERS

**Globe-trotting TIM BROOKE-TAYLOR recalls a
Pro-Celebrity Tournament in the exotic East.**

I have never gone along with Mark Twain's observation
that 'Mornington Crescent spoils a good walk.' So it was
with a light heart and head that I left the Clubhouse that
memorable morning. The desert sun beat down gloriously
on the freshly gleaming tarmac of the fareway of the Royal
and Ancient Mornington Crescent course that is the pride
of Dubai. I had been flown out the day before by Richard
Branston's Frigid Air, a trip made all the more enjoyable
when I was kindly upgraded to Freight Class.

I was in awe-inspiring company that morning. Our
foursome consisted of Sevvy Balham-Testros, Greg
Norwood (the Great White City), and the ten-year-old
prodigy St John 'Crickle' Woods. After a shaky start I soon
found I was holding my own, but that was only a sign of
nerves. I had a bogey on the third, but 'Crickle' helped me
to get rid of it, and play continued with mounting
excitement. My troubles really began on the seventh, when
I muffed an awkward dogleg and ended up bunkered just
short of the Parson's Green. Norwood played a delicate

chip out of Borough to Bank, and Woods amazed us all with a Tottenham Hale in one. Luckily I was given some breathing space when Sevvy missed a simple three-stop shot to the Nip, once again having problems with his Putneys.

I always say that the great thing about Mornington Crescent is that you don't play against your 'opponent', you play against the Game itself. That's what I always say, and I well remember the occasion when someone actually stayed long enough to hear me finish saying it, and even said 'Really?' before moving away. That's the kind of fascination the Great Game exerts, and many an evening I have kept a gathering open-mouthed, goggle-eyed, and restless with my detailed descriptions of some of my own more interesting exploits. I have often described an entire round in 75 to 93 minutes, and once I got through the Masters at Wentworth in 63 – a good 2 minutes below par! People talk of it still – not least myself! But I digress: back to Dubai…

I had just lofted a tricky Wood Green to Pimlico, and Greg and Sevvy were giving me a good-natured joshing over the idiosyncratic way I was filling in my scorecard. Brushing off the worst of the mud as I struggled out of the thorn-bushes, I saw that we had company on the course. Ahead of us film legend Sean Canary-Wharf and Jose Maria Ovalazabal were having a heated discussion over whether Sean was lost in the suburbs or not. Eventually Sean turned his back and dropped one behind him, which was hardly gentlemanly. We played through, and in no time we were on the 18th and victory was in my sights. But tragedy was to strike! I sliced my approach, and instead of sinking a simple Mornington Crescent, I ricocheted off Burnt Oak and landed in Waterloo! How they all laughed!

Bastards.

❖

NEWS FROM THE TERRACES

Pllchtwy ffan Nrtth Cymru!

14th March 2001 North Wales

Dear Mrs Trellis,
What excitement! We have
followed your doings for many a
year, and have now decided to
follow your great example and go
off in search of Mornington
Crescent! Yes, tho' this will mean
a trip to 'the Big Smoke', we plan
to visit London on the way back.

Plea[s]
use t[he]
Postc[ode]

Mrs Trellis
C/o North Wales
W41 Es

Auntie Vi is coming with us, so wish us luck! We'll bring you
back a shawl.

Yours sincerely, Sid and Nancy Terrace X
PS – We are your cousins who live next door.

LONDON

15th March 2001 LONDON!

Dear Mrs Trellis,
How right you were! The weather
is gorgeous and the people are
everywhere. Few sheep. Today we
'did' Oxford Circus to Bethnal
Green. Tomorrow we'll try Leicester
Square to Gunnersbury. Eh?!!
Auntie Vi has taken up with a
Beefeater – they are going
clubbing tonight, so we'll see!

Mrs Trellis
C/o North Wales
W41 E5

After all this North Wales will seem very nice and
pleasant. We'll see you when we get home.
Your neighbours, Sid and Nancy Terracex x

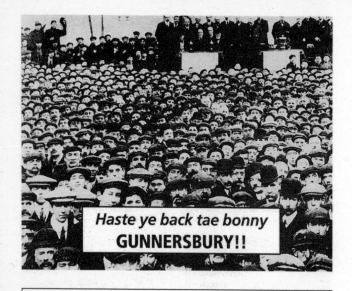

Haste ye back tae bonny
GUNNERSBURY!!

Dear Mrs Trellis,   16th March 2001 LONDON
Home tomorrow, thoroughly
disappointed! Gunnersbury not
nearly as beautiful as the
brochure. Auntie Vi's 'Beefeater'
turned out to be a cat burglar
and she ended up getting
mogged. Sid took his camera on
the tube, but didn't get many
views out of the windows. A man
stole it anyway. We ate kebabs in
the street last night - there's glamorous! - and the
minute we're discharged it's back home on the coach.
Your neighbours,
Sid and Nancy Terracex x

Please
use the
Postco

Mrs Trellis
C/o North Wales
W41 E5

CORRECTIONS AND CLARIFICATIONS

Some of the results printed in the report of the SCHOOLS 2000–2001 Season were inaccurate. An amended table follows.

Eaten Cottage – 0	1 –	Barrow & Wealdstone
Dollis Hill Primates – 0	1 –	Uppem 1st XI
Baker Street Irregular Stool – 1	0 –	Winchesty '73
Finchley Central Clots – 1	0 –	Charterflight Wanderers
Totteridge & Wetstone – 1	0 –	Marble Arce Approved
Chalk Fart Academicals – 1	0 –	Stewe
Sloane Square Ragers XI – 0	1 –	Aldwych filth form college
The Angel Proprietary School – 1	0 –	Turnham Groin
Cockfaster – L	L –	Shepherd's Bus *late kick off*
ꝫqwertyuiop – 0	1 –	Barons Court Seminally
Fairlop School for Little Lads – *bye*		Burnt Soak *closed for rebuilding*
Sir Arnos Grove's Upper Set – 1	0 –	King Edward School, Brimmingham
Foremarke Infects – 1	0 –	Ripton *own goat*
Arsenol – 0	1 –	Barking Academy of Damart
Seven Sisters Convenient School – 1	0 –	West Him
Gordonstoul – 0	1 –	Popper Primary
Shergar – 0	1 –	Chafing Cross modern
Holland Park Reprehensive – 1	0 –	Kilbum Incomprehensible
Wapping Tich – 0	1 –	Westmonster
Timbertops Touring Team – 1	0 –	Swiss Cottage Comprehesive
Morden Modem – 0	1 –	Ruddy 2nd XIV
Mile End 'Nutters' – 0	1 –	St John's Would
Tooting Bee – 0	1 –	Fatties
Elephant & Castle Spiral School – 0	1 –	Bundle
Mornington Crescent Casuals – 0	1 –	Nedsden
Mudchite – 0	1 –	New Barnet Hairdressing College
North Webbley – 1	0 –	New Cross *after extra tim*
Norse Woolitch – 1	0 –	New Cross Game
Kenton Cllge for the Sons of Gerry – 1	0 –	North Eating Special Needs
Kew Garments – F	F –	Leigh-on-Sex *failed to turn up*
Northwick Poke – 0	1 –	Manchester Uninvited
Kilburn Educational Felicity – 1	0 –	The Dralon School, Oxford
King's Cross Dressing Centre – 1	0 –	Ladbroke Gravy
King's Cross St Pandas – 1	0 –	Laid on *stewards' enquiry*
King's Cross Thameslink Cobbage – 0	1 –	Northfields Predatory
Latimer Roald Secretary – 1	0 –	Bush Street
Leicester Squat – 1	0 –	Lumpeth North
Northoot – 1	0 –	Kilburn Peek *reversed on appeal*
Lancaster Goate – 0	1 –	New Southgate *missed penalty*
Kingsboy Hugh School – 0	1 –	North Acton Combed Infants
Shrewsbunny – 0	1 –	Bosom Manor

MORNINGTON CRESCENT
2002 Fixtures and Fittings

January	**1st** – Order your 2003 MCC Almanac today! HALF PRICE! (offer closes 06.30am)
	8–18th – International Bot Show, Earls Caught
February	**14th** – St Valentine's day
	15th – Doghouse day
March	**1st** – St David's Day: have a leek
	12th – St Pancake's day
	17th – St Patrick's day: Shamrock season opens
	20th – Vernal Equinox born, 1735. Non-player
	23rd – Putney to Mortlake Boot Sale
	24th – British Summer Time begins
	25th – Late for work
	27th – Mornington Crescent Academy Awards (The Ongars)
April	**1st** – 'April Fool's Day' wins Grand National
	2nd – International Croix de Gare: Birmingham New Street Station
	5th – Smothering Sunday
	19th – Goodge Friday
	21st – Eastcote Sunday
	28th – First Sunday after Eastcote
May	**6th** – Bank Holiday
	7th – Bank Station open again
	25–29th – Chertsey Flower Show
June	**1st–9th** – British Open – Elephant & Castle
	10th – Queen's Official Birthday
	11th – Prince Philip's Official Bath-day
	12th – Trooping the Colour (presented by Davina McCall)
	16th – Father's day
	17th – Second-hand Tie Sales begin
	21st – Longest Day: C4, 2.35 am (Rpt)
July	**4th** – Royal Tournament (York v Wessex)
August	**12th** – Glorious Twelfth: Grousing season opens
	13th – Glorious Thirteenth: Grumbling season opens
September	**15th** – Prepare for 16th
	17th – Clear up after 16th

	22nd – Autumnal Eqinox: to Vernal, a baby sister (6lb 10oz)
	30th – Trooping the Colour (Rpt)
October	**15–18th** – Hearse of the Year Show: Olympia
	27th – Summer Time ends (put clocks back, unless paid for)
	28th – Clean socks
	29th – Finish cleaning socks
November	**5th** – Gay Fox night
	13th – Winter Drawers on
	30th – St Andrew's day: pamper a Scot
December	**21st** – Shortest day: hardly worth getting up
	24th – Cricklewood Eve
	25th – Anniversary of N.F. Stovold's first game in 1748 (beat Thick Bob Tully 1–0).
	31st – MCC Annual General Meeting, 8 till late, (Masonic Tearooms, Hull. Bring own chair)
	32nd – Extra day

Phases of the Moon

Full Moon

Half Moon

Builder's Moon

LIGHTING-UP TIMES
January–December 2002

1 First thing in the morning   7.30 am
2 After breakfast   8.15 am
3 With morning coffee   11.00 am
4 With lunchtime pint or aperitif 12.00
5 After lunch   1.45 pm
6 With afternoon tea   4.00 pm
7 With evening pint or aperitif 6.00 pm
8 After dinner   8.30 pm
9 Mid evening   10.00 pm
10 Before bed   11.50 pm

(Also at intervals during day according to preference)

(Times may vary)

PERSONAL COLUMN

Barking profess F, 31, seeks Wapping Monument to put her in Nip. BOX 75347

Bubbly F, 29, seeks man with High Barnett to explore her Western Approaches. BOX 394955

Victoria seeks Shadwell for walks, mountaineering, and triangulation. BOX 495968

Could my Elliptical Progression make your Kensal Rise? Let's find out. BOX 364482230208654

Burnt Oak WLTM Shepherds Bush for congruence or standard progression. BOX 58437

Queensway M, 25, GSOH, WLTM Poplar guy with impressive Embankment. Tower Gateway an advantage. BOX 462945

Outdoor type, 43, seeks non-smoking F, 30s, to share my Swiss Cottage and observe Albright's opening. BOX 69358

Triple Helsinki – 3 Finn students 20–25 seek solvent man with Mansion House. BOX 3945561

Seven Sisters, all saints, looking for Angel to illustrate Bartlett's Pass. BOX 89982

Barons court Kensington debs. 2 solvent Ms, 50–60ish, seek Sloane Square Sweeties (18–20) for companionship and standard deviation. A firm grip of Regency Rules will avoid misunderstandings. BOX 294

Chalfont and Latimer seek Maid of Ale. BOX 458667

Let's hit the town and Turnham Green. M, 40s, E London, seeks meaningful interchange with Metropolitan lady. NSOH. BOX 875378

No squares. M, 32 WLTM open-minded F with Oval face and own Pimlico. Object Marylebone. BOX 20459

Richmond! You contacted my box but I lost your number. Pls call again, can't wait to see Royal Oak. BOX 9495

TROUBLESHOOTING

Like Chess, Mornington Crescent is a game of enormous complexion, yet play is remarkably simple, and a game may be over in as few as 3 to 17 moves (the average number being only 24!). Now and again, however, players may find themselves in a situation where the game appears to have 'crashed', with no obvious remedy to hand. Many frustrating hours can then be wasted cursing and fuming – precious hours which could have been wasted playing the Game. The following simple tips, cheats, and wrinkles will help you to overcome such problems without recourse to expensive Help-Lines.

Game will not start

Checklist:
- Is there anyone with you who also wants to play the game?
- Has the plug been inserted? If so, remove it discreetly, and make yourself comfortable.
- Has the wall been laid out properly, with the funnel in place?

If none of the above problems apply, announce firmly 'Westbourne Park.' During the ensuing argument you will find the game will self-start.

Game will not end

Despite the satisfaction of winning, most players wish the game would never end. Nevertheless, after a year or two of continuous play, the gamesters may find they have other pressing business, or may require a comfort break. If the game then refuses to shut down, several courses of action may be tried:
- Say 'Mornington Crescent' whether you have prised open your laterals or not. Nobody will mind.
- Advance your Slappings, and sacrifice Bethnal Green. North's partner will be forced to trump.
- Feign a tidal wave.

Problems when transferring from the District to the Circle Line

Players sometimes find the Rolling Drive from below the line to the converse of Thesiger's Quadroit fails to connect. Play Aldgate three times in a row, which will open the hidden chamber below Chancery Lane. Follow the sewer pipe to the Shiny Bush, avoiding the Thwulgs, then kick the Goblin to collect the Hat of Invisibility and make your way to Level 4. After that it's Mornington Crescent in two.

Bullying

This can be a problem, but if properly carried out will provide much amusement for almost all concerned.

Escalators not working

This is an all too common fault. Players may be annoyed at missing their turn, but usually another turn will come along in about 7 minutes. Those with stout legs may opt for the stairs, while those with thin legs are advised to try Stannah's Elevation.

'Error' message displayed during the Mixed Game

It's annoying when this happens, but it is usually due to a lapse in etiquette. Remembering a few simple rules will avoid such disruptions to mixed play:

• Ladies first. Then the game can begin.
• Tooting Bec is considered impolite when there are ladies present, and should never be ignited.
• Ladies should remember to enter the room whenever a gentleman rises from his seat.
• Colliers Wood may be introduced, but not on a first date.

When all else fails...

The Mornington Crescent expensive Help-Line runs from Gospel Oak to Tuesday.
